Lay Caregiving

Diane Detwiler-Zapp
William Caveness Dixon

Fortress Press Philadelphia

Creative Pastoral Care and Counseling Series
Editor: Howard J. Clinebell
Associate Editor: Howard W. Stone

The Care and Counseling of Youth in the Church by Paul B. Irwin
Growth Counseling for Marriage Enrichment: Pre-Marriage and the Early Years by Howard J. Clinebell
Crisis Counseling by Howard W. Stone
Pastoral Care and Counseling in Grief and Separation by Wayne E. Oates
Counseling for Liberation by Charlotte Holt Clinebell
Growth Counseling for Mid-Years Couples by Howard J. Clinebell
Theology and Pastoral Care by John B. Cobb, Jr.
Pastor and Parish—A Systems Approach by E. Mansell Pattison
Pastoral Care with Handicapped Persons by Lowell G. Colston
Care and Counseling of the Aging by William M. Clements
Anger and Assertiveness in Pastoral Care by David W. Augsburger
Using Behavioral Methods in Pastoral Counseling by Howard W. Stone
New Approaches to Family Pastoral Care by Douglas A. Anderson
The Pastoral Counselor in Social Action by Speed Leas and Paul Kittlaus
Lay Caregiving by Diane Detwiler-Zapp and William Caveness Dixon

---

To our parents

Jeanette Caveness Dixon and Henry Longley Dixon

and

Nona Waters Detwiler and Edwin L. Detwiler

Library of Congress Cataloging in Publication Data

Detwiler-Zapp, Diane.
Lay caregiving.

(Creative pastoral care and counseling series)
Includes bibliographical references and index.
1. Lay ministry—United States. 2. Pastoral psychology. I. Dixon, William Caveness. II. Title.
III. Series.
BV4400.D47 253 81-66519
ISBN 0-8006-0567-5 AACR2

9028H81 Printed in the United States of America 1-567

Contents

Series Foreword

Let me share with you some of the hopes that are in the minds of those of us who helped to develop this series—hopes that relate directly to you as the reader. It is our desire and expectation that these books will be of help to you in developing better working tools as a minister counselor. We hope that they will do this by encouraging your own creativity in developing new methods and programs for helping people live life more fully. It is our intention in this series to affirm the many things you have going for you as a minister in helping troubled persons—the many assets and resources from your religious heritage, your role as the leader of a congregation, and your unique relationship to individuals throughout the life cycle. We hope to help you reaffirm *the power of the pastoral* by the use of fresh models and methods in your ministry.

The aim of the series is not to be comprehensive with respect to topics but rather to bring innovative approaches to some major types of counseling. Although the books are practice-oriented, they also provide a solid foundation of theological and psychological insights. They are written primarily for ministers (and those preparing for the ministry) but we hope that they will also prove useful to other counselors who are interested in the crucial role of spiritual and value issues in all helping relationships. In addition we hope that the series will be useful in seminary courses, clergy support groups, continuing education workshops, and lay befriender training.

This is a period of rich new developments in counseling and

psychotherapy. The time is ripe for a flowering of creative methods and insights in pastoral care and counseling. Our expectation is that this series will stimulate grass roots creativity as innovative methods and programs come alive for you. Some of the major thrusts that will be discussed in this series include a new awareness of the unique contributions of the theologically trained counselor, the liberating power of the human potentials orientation, an appreciation of the pastoral care function of the ministering congregation, the importance of humanizing systems and institutions as well as close relationships, the importance of pastoral *care* (and not just counseling), the many opportunities for caring ministries throughout the life cycle, the deep changes in male-female relationships, and the new psychotherapies such as Gestalt therapy, Transactional Analysis, educative counseling, and crisis methods. Our hope is that this series will enhance your resources for your ministry to persons by opening doorways to understanding of these creative thrusts in pastoral care and counseling.

This volume focuses on an area of significant need, challenge, and potential opportunity within the field of pastoral care—how to involve lay persons effectively in a congregation's ministry of caring. In the book, a psychotherapist and a pastoral counselor share their rich experience as co-trainers of lay persons doing caregiving in a church setting. They describe the methods they have used to enable individual caring and also ways of organizing and leading a training group for caregivers. They discuss the key role of the pastor in this training and give a theological foundation for lay caring ministries. They present ways of using self-care and preventive care groups for persons facing normal crises. The authors' brief verbatim illustrations help to illuminate the training methods they describe.

Within the context of the literature on training lay caregivers, this book has several fresh thrusts. It shows how to identify and give support to those lay persons already doing caring, spontaneously and informally, within a congregation. It describes ways of enabling lay caregiving in individual crises, prior to or separate from the task of organizing a lay training program. It recognizes, with refreshing realism, that most pastors initially resist the task of investing time and energy in enabling lay caregivers. But it also offers a convincing rationale for why it is so important that they overcome this resistance.

Diane Detwiler-Zapp is a psychotherapist at Family and Children's Services in Fort Wayne, Indiana. She also teaches feminist therapy at Indiana University-Purdue University-Fort Wayne. William Caveness Dixon is minister of pastoral care and counseling at the First Presbyterian Church in the same city. In addition he is on the staff of the Samaritan Pastoral Counseling Center and was director of training for Hospice of Fort Wayne.

In recent years it has become clear that pastoral care, in the New Testament perspective, is the function of a congregation as a caring community and not just of its ordained minister. All Christians have their own unique ministry, which no one else can fulfill. A crucial task of the clergy is to help release the tremendous undeveloped potential for caring in a congregation by providing ongoing training, coaching, inspiring, and undergirding of lay cargivers. In my experience, a church can double the breadth and depth of its ministry of mutual care by making lay caregiving a robust emphasis throughout the life of that congregation. This volume describes down-to-earth, practical methods of doing this.

I predict that this book will prove to be a valuable guide not only for pastors but also for the members of lay caring teams. It will be a useful resource for lay caregivers and their trainers in community programs such as those associated with crisis hot lines and hospice centers. I am pleased to have a book of such broad potential usefulness in this series. I hope that your energy level will rise (as mine did) as you encounter and implement its valuable concepts and methods.

HOWARD J. CLINEBELL

Preface

This book was born of our experience with lay pastoral care in the First Presbyterian Church of Fort Wayne, Indiana. More than seventy-five members of this congregation have received extensive training in lay caregiving since 1973. Their collective ministries have had a profound impact on the life of this downtown church of more than 2,500 members. An active community of lay caregivers is possible and even essential in a church of any size. We believe such a caring community embodies the shape and direction of the emerging church.

In our work with lay caregivers, we discovered that training was a surprisingly powerful experience. The growth and spiritual life of participants were greatly enhanced, and a valuable relationship of trust and understanding developed between pastor and parishioners. Although this book is directed primarily to pastors and church lay people, we believe the learning principles presented in chapters 6 and 7 can be applied to the training of lay caregivers in other settings. We have used them with hospice patient care workers, and envision their use with volunteers in service organizations such as Big Brother-Big Sister and public school paraprofessionals, and for clerical and support staffs in mental health facilities.

Our work in enabling caregivers has been exciting, challenging, and immensely rewarding. We wish you well in your efforts to build an effective, competent caregiving team.

We are grateful for the support, encouragement, and assistance of our families, co-workers, and friends. Ed, Kristy, and

Mara Zapp; Betsy, Katy, Jim, Karen, and Kelly Dixon have been patient, tolerant, and loving. Bob Collie, Alice Gillam-Scott, Barbara Wenbert, Charlie Worrall, and Margaret McCray-Worrall have laughed and cried with us. The Samaritans, the lay caregivers of our church, have learned and grown with us. Bob Jais's caring supervision and Howard Clinebell's careful editing were invaluable. Carolyn Hoshaw remained warm and giving throughout her typing and retyping of this manuscript. We are thankful for them all.

1. Rediscovering Lay Pastoral Care

> A church's caring ministry to the community's lonely, sick, aging, bereaved, shut-ins, strangers, institutionalized, and a host of other suffering human beings, can be tripled or more by involving trained lay people in pastoral work. When dedicated lay people become informal pastors to their neighbors, associates, and . . . church members, *they become the church*—the body of Christ serving those in need.*
>
> —Howard Clinebell

If you are like the pastors we know, you are busy, overworked, and scarcely have enough time to read a book such as this. Most pastors are experiencing increasing demands from their congregations for pastoral care at a time when their schedules are already overloaded and their emotional energies drained. If you find yourself in this pinch, we encourage you to look to the members of the church for help. We have found a vast storehouse of rich resources in the laity. This book will show you how to use this potential by enabling lay people to share the ministry of pastoral care.

Changing Your Perspective

We are not suggesting that you try to fit still another program into a weekly schedule that is already packed. What we are proposing is that you try a different approach, a new way of looking at your situation. Most of us attempt to find solutions to problems by repeating the same types of actions over and over with intensified determination. When these efforts fail we often become discouraged and frustrated. Watzlawick, Weakland,

and Fisch in their book on change† show that solving difficult problems requires that people abandon their usual approach and do something radically different. When someone comes to you reporting a pastoral need, your first thought might be, "What can I do?" or on a bad day, "Now what do I have to do?" We suggest that, instead, you ask yourself, "Is there someone else who can help?" Begin to see the people of the congregation as part of the solution instead of viewing their needs as a frustrating problem that you must carry alone.

Pastor Framiss had just finished his last committee meeting of the day when Jill Hammond, one of the members, approached him.

"Say, Fred, did you know that Maude Dipple broke her wrist this morning? She is home by herself now, and I think she needs some help."

"I'll stop by and see her tomorrow" was Fred's automatic response. He would have to wait until a decent hour in the morning to see her, and that would postpone his leaving for a meeting on the other side of town. This delay would require that he put off his hospital calling until that afternoon, and once again he would be late for dinner. His heavy sigh and weary eyes said to Jill that she had added to the burden of his day. This probably would discourage her from communicating such information in the future. Fred was concerned about Mrs. Dipple, but he went home feeling guilty, resentful, alone, overloaded, and not at all in control of his professional workload.

What if Fred had looked at things differently? He might have thought of Jill's report of Maude's accident as a potential *resource for help,* rather than another request for pastoral care that required his immediate action.

The dialogue could have sounded like this:

"I'm sorry to hear Maude broke her wrist. How did it happen, Jill?"

"She was sweeping her steps and slipped. As soon as she could get in the house she called me. We sit next to each other in choir, you know. I took her to the emergency room."

"I think it's marvelous the way church members reach out to care for each other. Maude is very lucky to have you."

"Well, thank you."

"What do you think needs to be done now?"

"Oh, I think she'll be okay. Someone ought to check on her. Maybe I could bring her dinner for a few days until she gets used to that cast."

"That's a lot of work for one person. Is there anyone who could help you?"

"Oh, sure. Margaret would be happy to help out once or twice. We can take care of it."

"Good. I have to be out of town tomorrow, but I'll give her a call in the morning before I go, unless you think there is an urgent reason for me to see her tomorrow."

"Well, I know she'd like to see you, but you probably don't need to go right now."

"Fine. Would you tell her that I asked about her and that I'll be phoning her tomorrow morning? I'll stop to see her in the next couple of days. Will you let me know if anything develops or you run into any difficulties?"

"Certainly."

"Thanks, Jill. What you're doing is important. You're helping our church become a caring community—what it ought to be."

This time, both pastor and parishioner go home with a lively spring in their step.

Overcoming Overwork

Symptoms of Burn-out

When we speak of the tired, overworked pastor, we are not suggesting that pastors have great susceptibility to "iron-poor blood" but that they have a high incidence of a malaise popularly called "burn-out."* This condition is usually experienced by people in occupations with heavy emotional demands. Burn-out is more likely to occur when such persons are overloaded with responsibility and lack support and interaction with others who are in the same kind of work. People afflicted with burn-out may complain of symptoms such as chronic weariness, fatigue or exhaustion, headaches, stomach problems, depression, insomnia, shortness of breath, or weight fluctuations. Pastors and others in people-oriented occupations may feel unappreciated and experience a dulled sensitivity to others. Feelings of cynicism, discouragement, and isolation are also common.

Prevention

Regular exercise, good nutrition, an occasional day of fun, and other methods of self-nurture are essential and helpful both in preventing and in alleviating burn-out. We believe that enabling lay participation in pastoral care also can be crucial in preventing burn-out among pastors. This can happen in several ways.

Delegating Responsibility

Delegation of authority and responsibility is one way physical and emotional overload can be avoided. The caring ministry of every vital church shares more pain, grieves more losses, touches more sorrow, and celebrates more joy than any one human can bear alone. As the laity becomes involved in pastoral care the emotional workload is borne on many shoulders. A lay person who provides care for only one person or family usually has more available time and emotional energy and is able to give more complete care than a pastor who feels responsible for ministering to the needs of an entire congregation.

Developing Support

Another preventive benefit for the pastor is emotional support. The first time lay caregivers visit a nursing home and are confronted by the sights, sounds, and smells that typify far too many of these institutions, they gain a new appreciation of the pastor who experiences this regularly. Mutual understanding and support begin to develop between pastor and parishioners, and among parishioners as they work closely in this shared ministry. Feelings of being isolated and unappreciated gradually are dissipated.

Receiving as Well as Giving

Pastors also can avoid burn-out by making certain they receive as well as give. Relationships that are equal, mutual, and reciprocal can be especially rich sources of nurture and should be a part of their personal and professional lives. As a pastor works with lay people and helps them enhance their caregiving skills, opportunities arise for all to be supportive and giving to one another. When lay caregivers support and nurture a pastor, an unbalanced relationship in which gratitude and appreciation are one-sided is avoided.

Ron Davis remembered how much he valued the presence and care of his pastor, Susan Williams, during the long grueling hours when his daughter was in surgery. He had expressed his gratitude to Susan on several different occasions, but words alone seemed inadequate. Somehow, watching Susan's tired face relax when he volunteered to visit Tom Jordan in the hospital helped Ron transform his gratitude into creative action. He no longer felt a sense of obligation to Susan, and they were able to relate more spontaneously to each other. Tom Jordan had an enthusiastic, motivated caller, and Susan Williams had an extra half-hour to work in her garden.

Why Involve the Laity in Pastoral Care?

Enabling lay people in the caring ministry of the church involves far more than "getting a few people to help the minister with calling." We believe lay pastoral care manifests the very nature and foundation of the church as a caring community with its common priesthood of all believers. It provides a place in the life and ministry of the church for those who hear and believe and want to put their faith into practice in a visible, tangible way. In most churches, the laity is already informally involved in pastoral care to some degree and could benefit greatly from the pastor's seriously and skillfully attending to the scriptural task of equipping "all God's people for the work of Christian service." (Eph. 4:12 TEV)

Reasons that Lay Pastoral Care Has Been Neglected

Pastoral care remains the most neglected area of lay participation in the church. Pastors have mobilized the talents of the laity in nearly every other area of church life. In most churches, lay people are found teaching in the church school, managing financial campaigns, working with youth, supervising the maintenance of buildings and grounds, actively working for community change, and leading in worship. Pastoral care, on the other hand, often has been seen as a ministry exclusive to the clergy. In the area of caregiving, lay people are often unrecognized, frequently unappreciated, and usually neglected. Yet they have an abundance of undeveloped resources for caring. Lay people are the greatest untapped potential of the church.

Out of Sight, out of Mind

In many instances lay pastoral care occurs outside the pastor's sight or awareness, and that can be a good thing. Even if the lay caring is seen, it often is not recognized or appreciated. In the following cases, lay caregiving was almost thwarted by a pastor's good intentions.

The Reverend Janet Mitchell had been serving Grace Church for more than a year and knew most of the congregation well. Dan Jancha, a sensitive church school teacher, stopped her one Sunday morning on his way to class.

"Janet, I saw old Sam Kibbey the other day. Ever since his wife, Freda, died, he's been feeling pretty low. When he was talking about her he started to cry. I just didn't know what to say."

Janet had conducted Freda's funeral about a month before and had visited Sam twice since then. He seemed to be grieving appropriately. The pastor had done her work well and felt current in her caregiving to him. Yet, when Dan spoke about Sam, she heard a voice inside her saying, "Here am I, Lord, send me." Fortunately, she did not act on this impulse.

If Janet had said she would go to see Sam, Dan may have felt, "I guess she doesn't think I'm doing very well or she wouldn't have to go. I wish she'd tell me what I should have said, but she probably doesn't think I'd understand. Maybe she thought I was telling her she wasn't calling enough. I was only trying to help."

Instead, Janet questioned Dan briefly to assess the situation and determine if Sam was becoming morose or unusually depressed. Dan's answers indicated that he was not and that Dan was, in fact, being very helpful in encouraging Sam to express and accept his grief. Janet did some informal teaching about facilitating grief work, gave Dan support, and validated his ministry.

"You've allowed Sam to express his feelings of sadness and loss, and that's exactly what he needs to do. I know how draining sharing another's pain can be. It sure is tough on me sometimes."

"Really?"

"Sure. Sam's a great guy. It's painful to watch him going through this. You're giving fine pastoral care, Dan."

"Well, I wasn't sure. I thought maybe I said something wrong."

"You probably said something just right and listened well, too. By the way, have you ever read Granger Westberg's book, *Good Grief?** I think I have a copy in my study if you'd like to borrow it."

Lack of Expertise

Not all pastors are as adept in this area as Janet Mitchell. In fact, most pastors initially find the task of enabling lay pastors awkward and unnatural. Their seminary and clinical training was directed far more toward teaching them to be caregivers themselves than toward helping them train others to give care. Although skill in caregiving is essential for effective ministry, this ability does not guarantee that one will be a successful teacher any more than being a good athlete assures one's abilities as a coach.

How Pastors See Themselves

Most pastors view themselves more as helpers than teachers. The responsibility they feel may carry with it a sense of ownership or exclusivity. "If pastoral care is my job, then I should be doing it, not someone else." Conscientious pastors may feel that by enabling others they are shirking their duty, that they are getting someone else to do their work. Even if they *believe* that pastoral care is a part of lay ministry, their feelings may cause them to resist implementing these beliefs.

Lack of Immediate Rewards

The ministry tends to be a profession with few tangible, visible rewards by society's standards. Salaries are generally low, and the chance for advancement by "promotion" often is limited. Pastors may be understandably more likely to seek the immediate reward of hearing "Maude Dipple really appreciated your call, Pastor" than to wait for the delayed gratification of building a congregation with a strong group of trained, active, and effective lay co-pastors.

Attitudes of the Congregation

Congregational attitudes and expectations also have hindered the development of lay caregiving. Most churches place a much higher priority on their pastors' providing direct care than on their ability to enable others to be caregivers. Although most churches expect their pastors to devote a significant amount of time to pastoral care, few include enablement as a part of their pastors' job descriptions. The very name "*pastoral* care" is usually understood to be care given by a pastor. The initial reaction of many church members to this involvement of laity may echo some of their pastor's own sentiments. "We hired the pastor to care for us, not to teach someone else how to do it."

Another more subtle but pervasive resistance to lay participation in the caring ministry grows out of the questionable theological doctrine of "salvation by observation." Holders of this tenet view Christianity as "a spectator sport" with the pastor functioning as the professional practitioner of the faith. This unfortunate heresy is one of the major underlying causes of an overworked clergy and an underinvolved laity. Recognizing lay people as caregivers is a direct challenge to this theological perspective, because it runs contrary to the belief that a good, hard-working minister can be their salvation. These people are confronted with the unavoidable responsibility of working out their "own salvation with fear and trembling." (Phil. 2:12 RSV) Considerable resistance is to be expected from such members, but the objections they raise and the obstacles they present may be "precisely the occasion for a realization" of this ministry.*

How the Pastor's Personality Can Get in the Way

The pastor's personality also can inhibit the use of lay people as caregivers, even though the overworked pastor gains from their involvement. Often the qualities that attract people to the ministry and make them effective are the very ones that get in their way of sharing this ministry.

How Pastors' Strengths May Act as Inhibitors

Independence and Autonomy

Most ministers have a well-developed sense of independence and autonomy.† The ability to work alone is essential because most pastors do not have support from co-workers or close, immediate supervision. Difficulties arise when the need for pastoral care exceeds the capabilities of one person to provide that care, which it does in any congregation of more than fifty members. The tendency to "do it myself," instead of enlisting the help of others, may mean that some of the work will not be done or the quality of care will suffer because of the pastor's exhaustion.

Sensitivity and Desire to Help

Two important parts of a minister's personality are a sensitivity to feelings and a desire to be helpful to others. Both are essential if one is to minister to the needs of the community. If these become too intense, they may undermine the pastor's ability to make rational, professional decisions about what should be done and who should do it.

One Sunday morning Jake Harold greeted his pastor, Ned Turner, with a jovial "How about lunch on Tuesday, Ned?" Jake's tired and drawn appearance did not match his somewhat forced greeting. His eyes seemed particularly sad. Ned was surprised and curious because Jake was usually fresh and alert, and lunching together was not an ordinary part of their relationship. Ned's sensitivity enabled him to recognize Jake's disguised plea for help. He felt an urgent desire to help but feared that if he accepted Jake's luncheon invitation, he might lose an opportunity to respond to Jake's immediate need. He also would have to cancel a meeting important to the future of the Sunday church school.

Ned knew himself fairly well and also knew that rushing to the rescue was not always helpful. He took a deep breath, silently acknowledged his conflict, and asked Jake what was on his mind. At first Jake said he was "just having a little problem, nothing serious." But when Ned asked if he wanted to say more, Jake poured out his pain. He had lost his job on Friday and was overwhelmed and frightened by his feelings of despondency. He didn't know what to do or which way to turn.

After half an hour of talking, Jake felt much better. The two set another day when they could discuss the situation further in the privacy of Ned's office. Ned suggested that he speak to Renee Mara, a member of the congregation and personnel director of a large corporation. Renee had helped Ned twice before when church members were out of work and was very understanding and gifted in aiding people in this circumstance. She was an expert at helping others write good résumés and was familiar with the business community. Jake agreed to call her the next day.

Ned's sensitivity and desire to help put him in touch with Jake's need. His willingness to share the task enabled him to provide immediate care and encouragement and to introduce a lay person into Jake's support system.

Action Orientation

Many people who enter the ministry are action-oriented. If they were not, they might be writing about injustice and suffering instead of being in a field in which "doing something" was required.

Crisis situations intensify one's natural desire to act. Two indicators that a crisis is in progress are the strong feeling of anxiety that the helper experiences and the thought "I must do something *now*." Spontaneous, immediate action on the part of the pastor can unintentionally inhibit those in crisis from using personal resources, prevent them from calling on available support from family or friends, and increase their feelings of inadequacy. The result is an exhausted helper and a discouraged, dependent person ill-equipped to meet the next crisis. The inclination and ability to act quickly could prevent a pastor from recognizing an opportunity to use the talents, life experiences, and caregiving skills of many church members.

High Goals

The typical pastor values achievement and has high goals. These qualities that often produce dynamic programs may inhibit the use of lay people as caregivers. The pastor for whom goals are extremely important and high achievement is a priority may be reluctant to trust "amateurs" to do this work. Wanting to succeed and to do well often makes the delegation of responsibility frightening because of the loss of control. If pastors become preoccupied with achievement, they may overlook the rich individual resources available in their congregations. Unfortunately, the pastor who places the highest value on quality pastoral care may be the very one who experiences the most difficulty in sharing with the laity the joys and satisfactions of this ministry.

How Pastors' Strengths May Act as Facilitators

We have discussed how changing an assumption or frame of mind is sometimes necessary before difficult problems can be solved, and have seen how some qualities of a pastor's personality can work against lay involvement. We are not suggesting that pastors discard independence, sensitivity, the desire to help, the ability to act quickly and effectively, or the value they place on achieving high goals. The change that is needed is one of perspective, so that lay people are seen as partners and a vital potential resource for pastoral care. Then pastors can use their personal and professional gifts to enable the laity in this ministry. Independence and autonomy will be essential in this undertaking because pastors will have to break away from the more established approach to pastoral care. The pastor's sensitivity and willingness to help will continue to be invaluable. When lay people minister to those in pain, they need care, coaching, support, encouragement, and sensitive confrontation. The ability to act effectively also will be extremely important. Someone will have to recruit and train lay people and help them learn to support, encourage, and grow from one another as they become pioneers in uncharted territory. The congregation will require education. Individual instances of pastoral care will need to be recognized and affirmed. The pastor may enlist lay people in the design, development, coordination, and administration of an entire system of congregational pastoral care. When a pastor offers immediate care it is like dropping a stone in the sand—the effects are noticeable but contained. Enabling several other people to be caregivers is like dropping the same stone in a pool of quiet water. Concentric circles spread and eventually change the whole character of the pool's surface. Implementation of this magnitude should satisfy the high aspirations of the most motivated pastor.

We hope this book will help change your perspective, and provide you with the ideas, encouragement, and inspiration to bring about a creative and dynamic change in any congregation.

2. Laying the Groundwork

> The dilemma of clergy/managers is to discover an authentic role for themselves in the midst of a "ministry of the laity" in which the laity *are* involved in the world—in their homes, on their jobs, in their schools, in their leisure, and in their volunteer commitments.*
>
> —Nancy D. Root

Enabling lay caregiving does not require beginning a major time-consuming program. It can mean little more than noticing those in the church who are already giving care and joining them in this ministry. There are two essential tasks in laying the groundwork to develop a system of lay care in the church.

1. Survey the needs of the congregation and community.
2. Identify the available resources.

Key lay people who know the church and community well can be an invaluable part of both of these tasks.

Survey the Needs

What individuals, groups, and institutions in the church and community need pastoral care? Consider what would happen if you were suddenly blessed by the addition to the church staff of a minister of pastoral care and calling. Whom would you suggest that this person visit?

Individuals

Take a moment and write down a list of people in the church

who could benefit from additional care. Who is taking the most pastoral time? Are there any who are neglected? Whom would you visit if you had more time? Add to your list those people who might be helped by having someone other than, or in addition to, yourself be the primary or secondary caregiver. Include individuals with special circumstances that make pastoral care difficult, such as those who speak a different language, live a long distance from the church, or have special needs resulting from alcohol or drug addiction.

Listing groups of people with special needs is a useful way to identify the pastoral needs of a church. Each community has its own unique circumstances that may call for pastoral care. Check this list and identify those who may need more care:

_______ elderly
_______ singles
_______ new residents/new members
_______ widowed
_______ unemployed
_______ veterans
_______ grieving and bereaved
_______ new parents
_______ deaf or blind
_______ mentally retarded
_______ low income and poorly housed
_______ critically and chronically ill
_______ immigrants, refugees
_______ disenchanted/inactive members
_______ lonely and shut-in
_______ migrant workers
_______ divorced, remarried, blended families
_______ families in crisis
_______ physically handicapped
_______ economically exploited
_______ victims of racial discrimination
_______ victims of sexual discrimination
_______ victims of age discrimination
_______ ________________________________
_______ ________________________________

Institutions

Almost every church is near at least one prison, hospital, nursing home or other people-serving institution. These institutions may serve the church members and also may have residents who are separated from their families, friends, and churches and could benefit from care provided by a local congregation. Add to your list those in nearby institutions:

_______ hospitals and clinics
_______ mental hospitals
_______ hospices
_______ veterans' homes
_______ schools for the retarded
_______ convalescent/nursing homes
_______ penal and correctional institutions
_______ colleges and boarding schools
_______ retirement housing and communities
_______ alcohol and drug rehabilitation centers
_______ group homes for children
_______ halfway houses
_______ ________________________________
_______ ________________________________
_______ ________________________________

Most pastors can find sufficient need for pastoral care in the community to use the time, energy, compassion, and faith of every member of the congregation.

Identify the Resources

In identifying the resources of a congregation, it is important to ask the right questions:

1. Who from the church is already giving pastoral care?
2. What is the quality of this care?
3. How can this caring ministry be identified, supported, and strengthened by training?
4. How can these efforts be validated and interpreted to the congregation?
5. How can the lay caregivers and the congregation be

helped to understand theologically that caregiving is the function of the whole congregation?

This identification process should be a natural continuation of your pastoral care ministry.

Discovering Potential Caregivers

As a part of his regular hospital calling, Pastor Jim Williams visited Nancy Chang, a member of the congregation who was recovering from minor surgery. After Jim spoke with her for a while, he noticed a collection of get-well cards on her bedside table.

"Have you had many visitors, Nancy?"

"Oh, a few, Jim."

"Has anyone from the church been to see you?"

"Amy Dawson's been here a couple of times."

"How did the visit go?"

"Very nice, actually. She came at just the right time yesterday afternoon."

"What do you mean?"

"Well, I guess I really needed someone to talk to, and she's so understanding."

"Amy must have been very helpful to you. I'm pleased that lay people in our church are caring for one another. I think that is very important."

Jim added Amy Dawson's name to his list of potential members of a pastoral care team. She obviously was interested in caregiving and knew how to listen. He also had identified Amy's visit as pastoral care and validated it to Nancy as important ministry.

Identifying Caregiving as Ministry

As a regular part of your pastoral visitation, you see members of the congregation who are engaged in the caring process. Because they are family or friends, they may not label their efforts as pastoral care. One of the theological tasks of a pastor is to identify the works of the Spirit. If you express your appreciation to parishioners for their good works on behalf of the church, you identify their efforts as ministry. This may help them to make a conscious connection between their positive motivations for caring and the values and traditions of their faith. They may recognize some previously untapped theological resources and then be able to celebrate the church as a caring community.

As she walked down the corridor of a nursing home, the Reverend Beth Cate met Joyce Bundy, a young church school teacher, whose frown and sagging shoulders suggested that she was troubled.

"Hi, Joyce."

"Oh, hello, Beth," Joyce responded with a heavy sigh.

"You look burdened."

"I am. I just saw my aunt. She is having one of her bad times."

"I was on my way to visit her. What's the problem?"

"She wants to go home again. She whimpers like a child and begs me to take her home. Right now I feel as if I can never go back to see her again."

"I'm sorry, Joyce. That must be painful for you."

"Yes, it is. I'd give anything if she could go back home, but she can't, of course. Even if she were physically able to, her house was torn down several years ago. She'll be all right, but she goes through these spells every now and then."

"She's lucky to have you."

"Well, I'm her only relative now."

"That can be a burden."

"Yes, but I'm glad I have the time."

"I'm grateful that you are doing the work of the church."

"The church has always been important to Aunt Carla."

"So has your ministry to her."

"I never thought of it as ministry before. I don't believe I could have assumed responsibility for her if it weren't for my faith."

"Our faith often opens us to strengths beyond ourselves."

"Yes. Yes it does, Beth. Thank you. Will you tell Aunt Carla you saw me and that I'll be back Thursday?"

"I'll be happy to."

Crisis situations often bring to visibility the natural caring instincts and skills of parishioners. Funerals, for instance, are an excellent setting to observe those who offer appropriate comfort and compassionate care. You can recognize potential lay caregivers in informal settings after worship, at a board meeting, or at the store or the post office. People who ask, "How's Martha doing?" or "I suppose you heard Jose Rellanos has to go to the hospital for tests?" demonstrate a caring concern. Ask them if they have spoken with the persons in need or if they have a special interest in them. You will probably begin a dialogue that will help you determine the extent of their abilities as caregivers and provide an opportunity to support their efforts as lay pastors.

Interpreting the Ministry to the Congregation

One of the most crucial tasks of laying the groundwork is validating and interpreting this ministry to the congregation. The validation process helps the church begin to understand that lay caregiving is a legitimate and vital part of the Christian faith and heritage, rather than the well-meaning busy work of a few pious do-gooders. It lends support to these caregivers by confirming that their work is important and valued and is included within the context of the church. Caregivers may now begin to share in mutual encouragement and support and exchange important information about those receiving care. Others may express a willingness to help where it is needed. The process of interpretation provides an arena to present a vision of what the church may become and to celebrate the current efforts of the church at work.

Sermons are particularly good vehicles for interpretation. You might begin with 1 Pet. 2:9 and preach on the priesthood of all believers, a concept central to the Reformation. The parable of the Good Samaritan (Luke 10:25–37), which depicts the lay person as the one providing the care, is particularly helpful in charging the congregation to "go and do likewise." James 1:26 suggests that the essence of "pure and genuine religion" is caring for widows and orphans. Jesus charges everyone with the ministry of caring for the needy in Matt. 25:31–46. He chose lay people, not priests, to be his disciples, and sent seventy-two of them out to minister (Luke 10:1–20). Paul encourages all to use their unique gifts (1 Cor. 12:1–11).

Articles in the church newsletter can be used to raise the congregation's consciousness about lay caregiving. Most pastors are asked occasionally to speak to church organizations on a topic of their choice. The subject "The Future of the Church" is always in vogue and is vague enough to permit you to reveal prophetic dreams of a church that creatively uses and enriches the caring skills of each of its members. Once this vision is integrated into your perspective, the process of interpretation will evolve naturally: in Bible study, confirmation class, adult education, and other pastoral activities. As the congregation begins to share this vision, the groundwork will be sufficiently prepared and the task of enablement can begin.

3. Helping It Happen

> When defining patterns of participation in pastoral care, the place to begin is not with some idyllic laity movement or a specialized clinical setting, but with the local church and one's own community.*
>
> —C. W. Brister

The Task of Enabling

Enabling is simply the process of providing what is necessary to make effective lay pastoral care happen. Most communities have a great need for additional pastoral care. All congregations have capable people who want to serve the church in a meaningful and worthwhile way and whose lives would be enriched by ministering to those in need. Enabling requires an alert pastor who can bring to light the ever-present warmth, willingness, and human caring latent in every church and can help connect these gifts to the needs of the community.

To lament the lack of lay caregiving is one thing; to bring into being a vital system of lay pastoral care in a church is another. An impassioned sermon on strengthening the fainthearted and supporting the weak may inspire members, but it also can leave them feeling guilty, inadequate, and frustrated if they do not have the means to put their inspiration into action.

Some members want to do more than make financial contributions to the church. The ministry of lay enablement helps these people put their faith into practice in more visible, tangible, immediate, and personal ways. It helps them "be doers of the word and not hearers only" (James 1:22). Enabling lay caregiving places Christianity in the hands of all its practitioners so that they may experience the responsibility, challenge, pain, and enriching rewards of living the gospel in a caring community. We recommend a five-step approach for doing this.

The A B C's of Enabling

Before you launch a major new program, we suggest that you simply try to involve lay caregivers individually as pastoral needs arise. This less formal approach requires a minimum of time and effort and permits you to exercise and develop your own enabling skills. The five tasks of enablement may be simply outlined.

Analyze and Assess Individual or Family Pastoral Care Needs

The first task of enablement is to analyze and assess the pastoral needs in a given situation. What is the problem? Whose problem is it? What hurts? What is needed? In *The Minister as Diagnostician* Paul Pruyser describes this diagnostic task as "grasping things as they really are, so as to do the right thing."* Recognizing a need and rushing off to help is not enough. Good intentions alone cannot provide competent, compassionate care.

As Pastor Paul Walters visited the hospital one afternoon he found Mike Pontz, a member of the congregation, in bed watching television.

"Well, hello, Paul. Come on in! How are things at the church?"

"Just fine, Mike. How are you doing?"

"Not too bad considering they're going to yank out my gall bladder tomorrow morning."

"How are you feeling about that?"

"I'm looking forward to it. I've put up with this heartburn long enough. Of course, it's a bit scary, but I guess I don't have much choice."

"What are you scared about?"

"Well, you never know what they'll find when they open you up. And I'm not exactly looking forward to the pain."

"I don't blame you."

"The doctor says there's absolutely nothing to worry about and he has enough pain pills to take care of me. But that's not what really concerns me."

"What does?"

"My wife Betty's worried sick. I can't get her calmed down."

"What's on her mind?"

"I don't know, but you'd think there was a fox in the chicken coop the way she's pacing around."

Pastor Walters had a long talk with Betty Pontz that evening. She told him that her father died during a gall bladder operation when she was sixteen. Mike's imminent surgery put her in touch with some old feelings. Paul Walters now had a better understanding of the pastoral needs of the Pontz family.

Analysis and assessment of a specific person's situation directs the entire enabling process. Trying to understand the nature of the problem gives birth to questions of how to minister to this person or persons in need. You may ask, "Is it appropriate to include a lay caregiver? For what purpose?"

Accurately describing the problem also helps you to explain specifically what you are asking if you decide to recruit a lay caregiver. When caregivers receive brief assessments of parishioners' circumstances, they are better able to explore the resources they might bring to those situations from their strengths, personal histories, and spiritual pilgrimages. They are better able to determine what they can do or be for the persons in need. As a pastor describes the needs of a recently widowed parishioner, a lay caregiver who has endured loneliness and grown from the experience may recognize how valuable this learning could be.

Analysis and assessment of a particular person's needs helps you and the lay caregiver avoid or minimize problems that develop when caregivers act too quickly in response to their need to help, instead of carrying out a thoughtfully considered approach to caring.

Begin Enlisting the Help of a Lay Caregiver

If you decide that lay caring is needed, the next step is to recruit a lay person to join you in this specific ministry. In choosing a person, look for someone who is

—loving:	warm, caring, sensitive, accepting
—empathetic:	understanding, open, a good listener
—genuine:	honest, authentic
—nurturing:	affirming, life-giving, able to help others grow and learn from life experiences
—trustworthy:	discreet
—stable:	emotionally and spiritually mature, strong, free from excessive stress
—accessible:	interested, willing, and available

Obviously you want to avoid selecting people whose personalities and personal problems would get in the way of caregiving. When you ask lay persons to help in the work of the church, you assume some responsibility for the quality of care that they give. In a time of need, people are particularly vulnerable. They should not have to deal with intrusive, insensitive helpers whose own needs or desire to be "helpful" overshadow their ability to provide care to others.

One important quality of a potential lay caregiver is accessibility. A person ideally suited for a given situation is useless if unavailable. Perhaps you have seen the tool especially designed for opening paint cans. It looks something like a cross between a bottle opener and a miniature paint scraper. This little gadget works superbly, except that you can never find it when you need to open a can of paint. So you usually end up using a screw driver, claw hammer, or the handle of a kitchen fork. The same principle seems to operate when enlisting caregivers. Even if you were able to picture the perfect person to minister to a particular pastoral need, that person might be out of town on the very weekend when needed most. The best person to enlist is not necessarily the most highly qualified but often is the qualified one who is most readily available and most easily accessible. Begin by recruiting the most obvious people, such as those who already have a relationship with, or an interest in, the person in need. Many times this person is the one who informs you of the problem. If you do not know of anyone who has a relationship with the person who is in the hospital, jail, or nursing home, ask, "Is there anyone you would like to have visit you?" Or ask yourself, "Who would benefit from providing pastoral care right now?"

Approach the person you select and present your understanding of the need. Then make a simple, direct, specific request.

After visiting with Betty Pontz, Pastor Walters went to a Stewardship Committee meeting. Esther Bixby called to him before the meeting began.

"How's Mike Pontz?"

"He seems to be doing pretty well."

"I spoke with Betty this afternoon, and she seemed very upset. She was really worried about Mike's operation."

"Yes, I stopped by to see her on my way here tonight."

"Oh, good. I just wish there was something I could do."

"I do, too. Would you be willing to help?"

"Sure, Paul. What do you want me to do?"

Contract a Cooperative Care Plan

Lay caregivers should participate in the answering of their own question, "What do you want me to do?" In order to provide competent pastoral care, lay people require a ministry that:

—they understand and that has well-defined limits
—they value and is valued by others (pastor, congregation, and recipients of their care)
—matches their abilities, gifts, and skills with the need
—has attainable goals or accomplishable tasks
—permits them to see some growth, progress, or at least the positive effects of their efforts

To do this, both you and the lay caregiver should formulate objectives and develop a care plan. Asking lay caregivers, "What do you think needs to be done?" encourages them to clarify and define the task, inventory their own gifts and skills, and begin to set some goals for themselves. Cooperative contracting blends the richness of the pastor's professional expertise and judgment with the caregivers' knowledge of their own interests, resources, and availability, and the needs of the troubled person. Deciding on a caregiving plan involves setting limits and establishing expectations rather than dictating a rigidly prescribed protocol. Who the caregiver is determines, in large part, what will be done. The ministry evolves with the creative, spontaneous, and redemptive power of the Holy Spirit, as one human being reaches out to another within the context of the caring community of the church.

Paul Walters had identified a potential lay caregiver. He allowed Esther to help answer her own question.

"The way I see it, Esther, Betty is the one who needs special help right now. What do you think could be done?"

"If I know Betty, she has all her dinners planned and prepared for the next week. And the kids are old enough to take care of themselves. But I'll check on that."

"Good. That would be helpful."

"Do you know if anyone is going to be with her during the operation? That's the worst part, waiting for the doctor to come and give you the news."

"You're right. I'll bet Betty would appreciate having someone there. Would you be able to go?"

"Sure. I'll give her a call tonight after the meeting. I know my morning is free."

"Please call me if you run into any difficulties. I'll be here at the church school teachers' workshop all morning, but it's all right to interrupt me."

Working together in the decision-making process helps to keep expectations realistic and prepares lay people to be better self-evaluators. When responsibilities are clearly stated, the chance for misunderstanding and disappointment is lessened, and the probability of a helpful and satisfying ministry is enhanced.

Demonstrate Your Support

As every pastor knows, pastoral care is sometimes a lonely, tiring, emotionally draining, and time-consuming task with few immediate rewards. It can be even more taxing for the laity, who lack the professional training and identity and who are not being paid for their time. Lay people as well as clergy are susceptible to "burn-out." Regular encouragement and support help to prevent them from "growing weary in their well-doing" and insure against discouragement and drop-out.

To make certain that lay caregivers know they are not alone in their ministry, assure them of your availability in case of emergencies. Inform them of your willingness to consult with them, provide guidance, and share opinions. Appreciate the importance and difficulty of their task and affirm their strengths and abilities. Explore with them the spiritual or ultimate dimensions of lay pastoral care. Be open to them as persons, to share their pain and disappointments, and to celebrate the hope and healing that result from their caring. The very act of asking them to be caregivers affirms that you are interested in them as persons and value their abilities. Lay people need support and encouragement throughout their ministries as much as you do.

Pastor Walters saw Esther Bixby after church.

"How did it go with Betty and Mike?"

"Oh, fine."

"Mike said you were very helpful to Betty."

"To tell you the truth, I feel awful. We didn't hear that Mike was okay until after ten-thirty. I thought Betty was going to crawl the walls."

"I'll bet."

"Do you know about her father?"

"Yes, she told me."

"That poor woman."

"You must have gone through a lot together. That's hard work."

"You bet. Especially when she asked me to pray with her right there in the waiting room."

"How was that for you?"

"Well, I'm glad it's over. Public prayer doesn't happen to be one of my strengths. But everything turned out all right."

"Sorry you were put on the spot. Sounds like you did just fine. Those are moments people don't easily forget."

Establish Continuing Contact

The final step of enabling is to make arrangements for ongoing communication between pastor and lay caregiver. Regular reporting is vital to a congregation's system of lay pastoral care, in order to:

—insure the opportunity for mutual encouragement and support
—review and evaluate the caregiver's efforts
—exchange current information and report significant change
—formulate new goals and objectives
—consider referral
—provide an occasion for learning new skills and experiencing personal growth
—deal with the feelings and issues that arise when a caring relationship ends
—let you know when you need to be more directly involved with the person receiving pastoral care

We suggest that the lay person assume responsibility for initiating these contacts. Simply ask, "Could you call me next Wednesday to let me know how things went?" (Until a regular routine of reporting is established, you may wish to make a note on your calendar to insure that contact is made.) This sets a realistic deadline without the lay person's feeling that you are "checking up." The lay caregiver wishing to clarify an issue or ask for help does not have to wait for you to call. Or you may prefer to have the caregivers write notes summarizing routine pastoral visits and place phone calls only when they have special concerns. Either way you are freed of the administrative responsibility of contacting what will hopefully become a growing team of lay caregivers.

The telephone rings.

"Hello, Paul? This is Esther Bixby. I'm calling about the Pontzes."

"Hi, Esther. Thanks for calling."

"You asked me to keep you informed about how things were going. Mike is taking long walks now. He has a checkup next week and if everything goes well, he can go back to work."

"Good."

"Yes, I think Betty is about ready. She's growling about having him around the house now. I think she's much better, too. She brought me a delicious chocolate cake the other day."

"Does it seem as if your work is about over?"

"Yes, I'm afraid so. Of course, I'll be relieved. It took a lot of time and energy. But I appreciate the chance to be helpful. With all my kids gone now, I like having something like this to do."

"Kind of hard to let go?"

"Yes. And sad. But good, too. I'm glad Mike and Betty are about back to normal. I'm going to miss my talks with Betty."

"I'm sure she will, too."

"Perhaps we can still get together—as friends. I like her a lot."

"Yes, and you are a good pastor. I hope I can call on you again."

"Sure, Paul. I'd like that. I really would. But give me a couple of weeks to recuperate."

Much of the success of an ongoing program of lay pastoral care rests on your openness and availability to lay caregivers. If this relationship deteriorates, lay people may begin to feel alone and ask themselves, "Who cares? Does it make any difference if I help or not?" When pastors are effective enablers, they begin to build a corps of dependable lay co-pastors who share their gifts in the caring ministry of the church.

4. Enabling Groups in Caregiving

> . . . we may then seek to train pastors who can enable the church to become a center of moral enquiry, a center for personal learning and growth, a center for human sustenance and nourishment, and a center for human reparation. The pastor will not have to do this alone, but will work to craft a social system that performs the above system functions.*
>
> —E. Mansell Pattison

Many of the same skills used in enabling individual caregivers can be applied to groups. Once you have worked with several lay caregivers and have become familiar with their abilities and limits, you may want to try working with groups for both efficiency and effectiveness.

Caregiving Teams

Most churches have certain areas that require ongoing pastoral care. These may include (1) hospital visitation; (2) evangelism and incorporating new members; (3) bereavement care; (4) visiting the elderly and shut-ins; (5) ministry to inactive members; and (6) identification of pastoral care needs while canvassing for annual stewardship pledges. Developing a team of lay caregivers trained and organized to minister to these specific needs can be helpful. One or two teams might be formed to divide these tasks, or an area of priority might be established. In a large congregation a separate team could be formed for each.

Advantages of Caring Teams

Caring teams have many advantages. Recruiting becomes primarily a one-time effort. Group orientation and training saves considerable time and provides opportunities for caregivers to learn from each other. (See chapters 5 and 6 for more information on training.) Once a team is established and assignments are scheduled, the program is nearly self-sustaining.

Much of the maintenance and administration can be handled by a lay person. Weekly or biweekly meetings of participants will facilitate the mutual support, encouragement, and personal growth that are vital to ongoing programs of lay pastoral care. The group will form an identity and develop a history that will help shape and define its ministry. As the team of lay caregivers becomes established and more visible, the congregation will begin to recognize and accept them as a regular part of the work of the church.

Set Goals and Outline Plans

Decide the area of pastoral care on which you would like to focus, and establish how lay people could participate. Be as specific as possible. For instance, your goal might be to provide continuing lay pastoral care to members of your congregation who are hospitalized. Perhaps you regularly call in the hospital on Monday, Wednesday, and Friday, and you would like to have lay people call on days you are not there. Perhaps you will be able to think of eight people in the congregation who have the ability to provide this care and who might be willing to do so.

One way to organize them is to have three of these people volunteer to visit the hospital once a week for a month on assigned days of the week. Three others would assume this schedule on alternate months. The two remaining people would be available as substitutes in case of vacations, illness, or schedule conflict. One of these people would serve as coordinator of the team.

Team members would telephone the hospital before their visits to determine who, if anyone, is there from the congregation or denomination. They would call the church office after their visits to give updated reports. They would also call the lay co-ordinator to arrange for substitutes if they were unable to make their visits. All members of the hospital visitation team would meet once a month to discuss any administrative problems and to provide mutual support, continuing education, and personal growth. It would be preferable for this meeting to be held near the end of the month so that information about currently hospitalized members could be passed from one group to the next.

Enlist a Co-ordinator

Decide which one of your potential caregivers would work best as a team co-ordinator to handle the administrative details of maintaining this new program. Explain your plans to establish a caregiving team and ask if this person would be willing to work with you on this project. If so, share your ideas and work together to design the program. Use the co-ordinator's ideas wherever possible. As lay people participate in the planning, they develop a sense of ownership, responsibility, and loyalty, helping them to give and receive more from their ministries.

Recruit Potential Caregivers

As you and your co-ordinator develop a list of possible caregivers, remember that co-ordinators usually work best with people they know, trust, and respect. Teams that include women and men, various age groups, and people with different life experiences provide richer resources.

Set a date for an informational meeting to allow potential team members to meet and get a better understanding of what is expected. Next, divide the list between the two of you and recruit each potential helper individually. Briefly describe the program and tell the prospective members why they were selected as possible participants. This shows that you value them as persons, suggests some of the strengths needed for the task, and affirms their potential. If they show interest, invite them to the informational meeting.

Getting a Commitment

The informational meeting offers an ideal setting for you and your co-ordinator to present in detail the nature, purpose, and importance of the caregiving team. Encourage potential members to respond to your proposal and provide an opportunity for them to discuss various aspects among themselves. Ask for their suggestions and give their ideas serious consideration.

Specifically describe the various tasks and responsibilities assumed by members of the caregiving team. Negotiate a date and time for a regular team meeting, and reserve the first meeting for orientation. Next, set up a schedule and ask for volunteers to commit themselves to visit on their assigned days, beginning the month after orientation.

Try not to pressure people into volunteering. Allowing anyone who wants to drop out gracefully at this point may save you considerable time later. Those people who are unsure or who have "possible schedule difficulties" may be willing to serve as substitutes. If you have far more volunteers than you need, you may decide to use three teams or perhaps may consider branching out by visiting the elderly or involving people in other areas of lay pastoral care.

Orientation Meeting

The purpose of an orientation meeting is to help lay caregivers as they begin their ministry. You may wish to ask the hospital's chaplain, director of nursing, or social worker to provide the team with an introduction to the hospital. They probably will be pleased to speak to your group to describe the hospital's policies and procedures, present some general guidelines for visitors, and perhaps offer a brief tour. This also will help educate the hospital personnel about the value of lay caring.

Give the members of the hospital visitation team clearly written instructions that outline their responsibilities and a copy of the schedule that shows when they are to visit. Providing a list of names, addresses, and phone numbers of team members is also helpful. Discuss the importance of confidentiality with the group and help the members understand why it is essential. If you have other definite instructions to offer, do so at this time. We usually keep specific instructions to a minimum because we prefer to have caregivers develop their own styles.

Provide a time for team members to talk specifically about their fears and anxieties. After these feelings have been expressed, discussed, and affirmed as natural, the group is freer to celebrate its excitement about this new venture.

Team Meetings

Monthly team meetings provide times of nurture, support, and learning. Even though some groups may want to talk all evening, these meetings are usually most effective when they are limited to ninety minutes. For the benefit of those who soon will be assuming duties for the next month, some of the agenda should be reserved for sharing information about currently hospitalized members. Participants might exchange helpful information on a useful book or article, a new discovery in a medical procedure, where to park, or the progress of someone experiencing a long recovery after being discharged from the hospital.

The most enriching part of these meetings is the opportunity for the caregivers to share feelings about their ministry and to learn from their experiences. This provides a setting for pastors and lay co-pastors to support each other as a genuine caring community. These experiences give birth to new self-understanding as team members reflect on life-and-death issues and struggle with the concrete theological questions that arise out of their task. Team members grow as persons as they come to know themselves and each other more fully. The personal problems that naturally come to the surface in an atmosphere of intimacy should not be brushed aside, but you should encourage the group to keep its primary focus on its ministry. Training experiences such as role plays can help caregivers learn new ways of caring and experience how they feel receiving care.

Maintenance of Caregiving Programs

Public recognition and congregational support are especially important in the initial phase of enabling a caregiving group. Newsletter articles and bulletin announcements that describe the program and list the participants are useful in the beginning.

Later you may want to have an annual recognition of lay caregivers during worship. The co-ordinator should keep close contact with team members in the first few weeks to foster a sense of responsibility and accountability and to detect possible problems early. Pastors should make a special effort to pass along positive feedback to members of the caregiving team: "I saw Bruce Wimmer at the hospital the other day, and he mentioned that he really appreciated your call." Notifying lay caregivers of the death of a patient they have been visiting is important. If they have become close to that person, they have their own grief work to do. They also may have established relationships with the family, relationships that will be supportive during the bereavement.

People who express interest in joining an established caregiving team can be given a brief private orientation and printed materials describing the program. At first they may be placed on the list of substitutes and invited to attend the monthly team meetings. In this way, new team members may be incorporated into this ministry at their own pace. You might ask new and old members how they feel about the group's being changed by the addition of new members.

Self-Care Groups

One of the most effective ways to enable lay caregiving is through self-care groups. People who have experienced a particular problem, hardship, or pain can be great resources for others going through similar difficulties. Alcoholics Anonymous, Recovery Incorporated, the Cancer Society, and the Stroke Club have been very successful in forming groups of people with common experiences to care for each other. Pastors have a unique, privileged awareness of the lives and histories of their parishioners and can use this knowledge to bring together people with similar struggles. If you have two widows in your congregation, you have the start of a self-care group. There may be others such as (1) divorced/divorcing individuals; (2) those parenting aging parents; (3) homosexuals and/or their families; (4) remarried and blended families; (5) parents of exceptional children; (6) bereaved/grieving; (7)

people experiencing societal oppression such as sexism, racism, and ageism. These groups may be led by one member of the group or the leadership may be shared or rotated. The pastor may serve as a consultant.

People who have experienced tragedy and survived can offer hope to others simply by being there. A young couple grieving over the death of an infant began to see the possibility for their future when they spoke with another couple who also had lost a child but now had other healthy children. A common bond between people presumes an understanding and appreciation of each other's situation. This facilitates growth without a long period of trust development. Sometimes people turn aside the efforts of others to help because "you just can't understand." Sympathetic understanding, however, permits a certain toughness and confrontation that can break through such arrested growth.

Tim lost his leg in a boating accident. He had withdrawn from his family, friends, and the hospital staff. He was not doing well medically. His pastor asked Scott Davis, who also had lost a leg, to visit Tim. Scott went to the hospital and danced a jig beside Tim's bed, defying him to identify which one of his legs was artificial. From that moment, Tim began to get well. Scott's own loss gave him the permission and power to say to Tim, "I *do* understand. Now rise up and walk!"

One-to-one caring can be helpful if the caregivers' own emotional wounds have healed sufficiently and their loss or pain have been integrated into the growth patterns of their lives. Self-care groups have the advantage of offering the perspectives of several people. This can provide group members with more alternatives and varied choices. It also insures against a narrow, singular point of view that may insist, "I went through the experience this way; therefore, you must do it the very same way." Self-care groups in the church offer a context in which people can struggle with the meanings of their histories, experience the comfort and healing power that are promised "when two or three are gathered together in my name," and benefit from the redemptive process of being cared for as they care for others.

Caring Through Growth/Enrichment Groups

Lay people also may participate in "preventive" pastoral care through groups organized to foster growth. Growth/enrichment groups provide care by helping people explore new possibilities for life in abundance and by developing their potentials as whole persons. They help people form support networks that may encourage and nurture them through difficult times. Pastors may bring together:

1. New parents wanting to learn parenting skills and to grow with their children
2. Single adults seeking companionship and celebration of singleness
3. Those seeking deeper, richer, more intimate marriages
4. Women or men who are questioning, or feel limited by, traditional roles, and who wish to explore new ways of relating
5. Older adults wishing to share meaningful ways to use their wisdom and experience
6. Those committed to changing institutional oppression, promoting ecological stewardship, or creating community wholeness*

This concept of pastoral care is not new to the church. Many Bible-study groups have been serving this function for years. When people meet for the explicit purpose of nurturing each other's growth within the context of a caring community, lay people will experience exciting new dimensions of their pastorhood.†

Enabling Pastoral Care in Existing Organizations

Existing church groups are another valuable resource for lay pastoral care. They have the advantage of an established structure, leadership, and a system of communications. Women's circles, Sunday church school classes, choirs, and senior high basketball teams all have ongoing relationships with their members. These groups feel some responsibility for one another and care for one another as a matter of course. You can be helpful by supporting and encouraging these efforts. Perhaps the most important role of pastors in enabling existing organizations is to inform group leaders when one of their members is in need.

On returning from the hospital Friday afternoon, Pastor Laura Hayes telephoned Walt Blakely to tell him that a member of his junior high class had just undergone an appendectomy and would not be in class Sunday morning. The pastor's call suggested that she valued Walt's work with the young people and that she was interested in church school attendance; it also opened the door for lay pastoral care. Walt said that his class might like to make a giant get-well card for their missing member and then asked if there was anything else he could do. Laura answered that she believed the young woman would be well enough for visitors in a day or two and encouraged him to call.

As a congregation's individual members and groups realize their responsibility and potential for each other's healing, wholeness, and growth, the church will begin to become a caring community of pastors.

5. Enriching Lay Caregivers Through Training

And some kind of help
Is the kind of help
That helping's all about.
And some kind of help
Is the kind of help
We all can do without.*
—Shel Silverstein

The extra time and energy you devote to enabling others in caregiving can greatly increase specific instances of pastoral care within a congregation. The reality of limits does exist, however, even for the most skilled enabler. Sermons still have to be written, administrative duties remain, and the increasing needs of congregational members are ever present. As you become more successful in involving members in caregiving, the opportunities and need for training increase.

Why Training?

Many pastors find training to be one of the most rewarding, exciting, and challenging aspects of enabling lay caregivers. Training should create enriching, nourishing, and growing experiences to help caregivers give competent, compassionate care.

Willard C. Richan, in his article on training lay caregivers, states that "there are serious risks involved in intervention in other people's lives by persons without professional training. Inadvertently the lay person may do great harm in the guise of helping."† A recent loss, crisis, illness, or profound sense of loneliness may leave a person emotionally vulnerable. A well-meaning visitor who adds to that person's frustrations may cause more damage than mere annoyance. A grieving widower may find his despair deepened by the caller who smiles and says, "Well, things aren't so bad; at least you have your children." The loneliness and isolation this man feels may be intensified as he experiences the alienation of not being understood. Good intentions are not enough! Training helps to transform good intentions into helpful interventions and to eliminate "the kind of help we all can do without."

People who volunteer to help others usually want to do well. They do not want to be embarrassed by feeling awkward or saying the wrong thing. Even though they may be skilled caregivers, volunteers need at least a brief orientation to learn what is expected of them. This introduces them to the administrative procedures of receiving assignments, reporting progress, and making referrals. Most lay people will welcome the opportunity for more extensive educational experiences to help them minister more effectively.

Various Forms of Training

The primary task of training is "to minimize the risks of harming people in need of help," and to "maximize the potential for helping."* We have found that meeting with more than one person to discuss pastoral calls is beneficial in many ways. In addition to the obvious time-saving factor, lay caregivers learn from one another and offer mutual support. The various examples of pastoral care they bring provide real-life data for learning. The structure of a designated meeting time adds a more formalized touch that affirms the learning process and strengthens the commitment of the participants.

Training Events

You can nurture and enrich lay caregivers by providing

various training workshops, seminars, retreats, lectures, and discussion groups. The possibilities are many:

1. During Lent, offer a series of weekly lay pastoral care seminars on such topics as "Death and Dying," "Ministering to the Elderly," and "Understanding Cancer."
2. See if there is a physician in your community who is sensitive to interpersonal and emotional matters and would be willing to tell lay caregivers about the unique aspects of pastoral care to people who have suffered heart attacks or strokes.
3. Invite the chaplain or social worker of a nearby jail or prison to present a workshop on prison ministry.
4. Plan a film forum on issues in caring, together with a discussion of lay pastoral care, using movies such as *I Never Sang for My Father* and *Teenage Father*.
5. Use a television program or drama like "The Shadow Box" as a starting point for a discussion on caring.

Making Resources Available

An easily accessible pastoral care library or resource center can be helpful for those who want to learn on their own. In addition to books such as those listed in the Annotated Bibliography at the end of this volume, many good pamphlets are available from local hospitals, mental health agencies, Alcoholics Anonymous, Family Service Agencies, and your own denominational offices. An occasional book review in the church newsletter will stimulate interest and remind people of what is available in the pastoral care resource center.

Encouraging Outside Training

Educational opportunities for lay caregivers can be found within driving distance of most communities. Funeral homes, for instance, occasionally sponsor workshops for pastors on grief and bereavement. These are often open to interested lay people. Most pastors receive numerous brochures and fliers advertising such events. Why not reserve a section of your bulletin board for them so that members of the congregation may see what is available? Outside training events affirm the validity of what is being done within the congregation and bring in new ideas. They also create enthusiasm for learning.

Comprehensive Training Programs

Comprehensive training programs are long-term, in-depth training experiences that can offer more thorough preparation for caregiving than brief training events. Although they require more work on your part and a much greater commitment from lay people, we believe that the results of the training as well as the rewards of the process are well worth the effort. In fact, we have found that a comprehensive training program can become one of the most meaningful and important experiences in the life of a church and its members.

Packaged Programs

Some pastors have created training programs that have been so successful that they have collected their materials and marketed them so that other churches could benefit from them. The "Stephen Series," for example, is a general training program for lay caregivers. LEAD workshops, designed primarily for training lay people to visit inactive members, offer helpful material on active listening skills that would be useful in most pastoral care situations. Both of these programs will send further information upon request.*

Planning Your Program

We believe that training programs are most effective when they are designed to meet the unique needs, interests, and resources of a particular congregation. The model offered here is based on our experience over the past several years. We suggest that you adapt it to your own situation.

We regard a model as a way of beginning—an evolving, growing, changing, useful way to accomplish a specific desired outcome.† Our model was designed as a method to recruit, train, encourage, and enable lay people to provide competent, compassionate care. Our church is large enough to offer this training every fall. Although our basic structure has remained fairly constant, individual aspects are still evolving and we are still learning. As we recognize that certain learning experiences are not effective, we discard or redesign them.

We encourage you to begin with this particular model and to imagine how it might work in a specific congregation. What outcome is desired? What needs to be done? What resources are available? What parts seem practical and feasible and what parts do not? Our purpose here is simply to share our experience and to encourage others who dream of an active, caring community in which people help and nurture one another through times of personal growth and crisis.

A Training Program Model

Choosing A Time

We begin by establishing dates for the training program and reserving those times on the calendar. We choose a period when we can set aside twelve to fourteen consecutive Wednesday evenings from 7:30 to 10 o'clock (Sunday afternoons might work as well). This is a substantial investment of time, but we have found that once lay caregivers have committed themselves to the program, absenteeism is surprisingly rare. Usually this block of time has been from mid-September through mid-December. We have tried biweekly meetings but have discovered that participants in these sessions lost some of their enthusiasm and sense of continuity. They found sharing more difficult than those who met weekly.

Recruitment

Several months before the training starts, we begin putting articles in the church newsletter to introduce the program and to explain some of its concepts. Immediately after Easter, we initiate a recruiting period that is completed before the summer vacation months. First, we invite people to an informational meeting held around the first of May. Open invitations are issued by word of mouth, posters, personal letters, and announcements in the church bulletin. We recruit people to come to the *informational meeting only* and not for the training program itself. There are several reasons for this:

1. An open invitation reduces the possibility of people feeling hurt or excluded, or thinking that the pastor is playing favorites.
2. By issuing an open invitation, you may attract capable people you had not considered.
3. This training requires so much time and energy that people need a chance to consider it thoroughly before making a commitment. If people are confronted too soon with the requirements, some may say no before they discover the possible benefits of the program. People are more likely to come to an informational meeting to learn about an exciting new challenge in the church than they are to sign up for a program of this magnitude without being thoroughly informed.
4. Many people are more likely to pursue their interest in training if they see others with the same questions and hesitations that they have and if they catch the enthusiasm that can be generated at such a meeting.

Screening

How do you keep "the church gossip" out of the training program? The personality, dependability, or current emotional state of some people make them less than ideal caregiving candidates. The method we use for screening is almost entirely "self-selection." By our explaining as clearly and as thoroughly as possible what is expected of lay caregivers and what they may expect of us, most people who would not be suited for this experience exclude themselves. The commitment required for this kind of program screens out most of those with only tentative interest and sustains learners through the demands of training.

At the informational meeting, we hand out a brochure that describes the program, lists the dates, and states the fee (set primarily to cover the cost of a retreat). We also ask everyone who is interested to complete an application and be interviewed. These procedures show that there is an entry process. They force interested lay people to struggle with their qualifications and motivations for training. The application asks for the following information:

1. A statement describing how they became interested in the program, how they expect to profit by the experience, and why they want to participate.
2. A brief description of an event in which they helped someone and an evaluation of their work as a caregiver.
3. A list of educational experiences, books they have read, seminars, retreats, or workshops attended, and life experiences that will contribute to their work as a lay caregiver.
4. An autobiographical sketch. This section offers them an opportunity to tell us who they are. They may include significant events that have contributed to their motivation to care for others.
5. A brief outline that describes the kind of pastoral care they would like to do. (Each caregiver is expected to make at least one pastoral call per week during the training program.)

The interview explores these areas in greater depth. People who have come this far in the process have demonstrated substantial motivation and commitment. If there are some doubts about their abilities and the appropriateness of their receiving the training, this interview is the time to discuss these issues. Occasionally we have requested that people wait a year until current stresses in their lives have lessened and they have more energy to give to others. In a few instances, we have helped applicants discover areas in which they need more work and have suggested that they reapply when they feel some progress has been made. In the rare instances in which self-selection does not work, we tell applicants that we believe they are not ready at this time or we ask them to return for further conference. These experiences, though difficult and painful for us, have almost always had positive outcomes. This interview approach protects those in need of pastoral care from someone like "the church gossip," who may also disrupt or undermine the training process. We have found that confronting people with problems at this point is much better than trying to work with or around them throughout the training program.

Each of those accepted into the program is sent a letter of congratulations and invited to an orientation meeting about the first of June. At this meeting the lay people celebrate their acceptance and start to form a group. We give them each a bibliography and encourage them to read at least one book during the summer. We also suggest that they begin to consider more specifically what they want and need to learn.

Weekend Retreat

The training begins with a weekend retreat. We choose a camp or conference center that is away from the day-to-day responsibilities of home, church, and job, so that we will have a large block of uninterrupted time. This is such an extremely important part of the training that we feel attendance is mandatory. The hours spent from Friday evening through Sunday afternoon constitute a large portion of the total program. The retreat helps to initiate the important processes of establishing trust and building relationships that are so crucial to learning, growing, and receiving support during the training and beyond. The lay people assess each others' strengths and weaknesses and begin to share experiences together as a group. They assume their roles as "learners" and caregivers and begin to explore and define the new relationship with their pastor in the "supervising" role. (This is explained more fully in chapter 7.) Caregivers acquire some new skills to help them in their ministry and begin to recognize and affirm the skills they already have.

Weekly Meetings

Weekly meetings are divided into two parts: the supervisory group and the lay pastoral care seminar. There is a fifteen-minute coffee break between the two. In the supervisory group learners discuss their visits, problems they have encountered, and insights they have gained. The agenda and issues evolve out of the needs of the learners. The seminars, on the other hand, present a variety of materials and learning experiences that we have prepared. Topics vary from year to year according to the special needs and interests of each group. They may include:

1. Listening: how to hear what is said both verbally and nonverbally.
2. Responding: learning and practicing helpful responses.
3. Clinical writing: how to present and learn from written accounts of pastoral calls.
4. Crisis intervention: recognizing a crisis and knowing what to do.
5. Referrals and resources: information about community resources and learning when to refer.
6. Illness and wellness: the dynamics of health and ministry to the sick.
7. Understanding personality: a growth-oriented, holistic approach.
8. Family systems: ministering to people within the context of their relationships.
9. Growing older: understanding the significant passages of aging.
10. Loss and grief: the grief process and its common causes (including death, divorce, retirement, and family changes).
11. Death and dying: caring for the dying and the bereaved.
12. Termination: exploring common themes and feelings associated with endings.

Ending the Training Experience

At the conclusion of the weekly meetings, each learner writes a final evaluation. We also prepare an evaluation of each learner and discuss these in a final interview.

The training experience traditionally has concluded with a banquet. This celebration usually has been held at the church. Sometimes spouses or friends have been invited, other times not. Speeches are made and certificates are presented. Often the lay people have their own "awards" to give. These often take the form of a humorous history of the training experience with some playful "roasting" of the leaders. Sometimes the evening has concluded with a moving Communion service. Whatever form this celebration takes, emotions are mixed because a very significant, meaningful, and growing experience is ending.

6. Some Helpful Things to Know About Training

In Zen Buddhism, responsibility for change is laid entirely on the disciple. . . . The Zen Master is a Socratic midwife to the person who seeks the truth. The Master does not teach truth but becomes the occasion for the discovery of truth. In midwifery the woman gives birth to her own baby.*

—Donald K. Swearer

Basic Assumptions

The specific form of any training program evolves from the basic beliefs of its designer. The following principles have guided our efforts to create the most effective training experience:

1. Three elements are essential in training lay caregivers: personal growth, improving caring skills, and integrating theological beliefs and concepts into the practice of caregiving. Training should not neglect any one of these elements, and ideally they should receive equal emphasis.
2. Learners are responsible for their own education. Leaders should not decide for the learner: "This is what you need to know." Instead, the learner struggles with the perplexing questions: "What do I need to learn? How will I learn what I have decided I need to know? How will I evaluate myself to know that I am learning?"

3. Learning involves personal experience that is reflected upon, evaluated, and then integrated into the life of the learner.† Learning evolves from personal experiences. The learner thinks about these events and asks, "What happened? What was helpful? What was not helpful? What can I learn from this? How would I behave differently if I could repeat the experience?" These "active learners"† engage in an ongoing dialogue between theory and practice, as they reach a greater understanding of themselves.
4. A learner needs a caring community of other learning caregivers. Sharing this learning experience with others is helpful. A group of peers provides mutual support, understanding, confrontation, and encouragement.

Essential Elements of Training

The most effective training affirms the wholeness of each caregiver by offering a variety of learning experiences. We are created as a unity of body, mind, and spirit. The more our learning encompasses all aspects of our being, the more whole we become.

Personal Growth

Training should provide an atmosphere that encourages learning and nourishes the ongoing growth process of each caregiver. To neglect this fundamental aspect is to suggest that people are fixed entities rather than changing, evolving beings. John Powell, in his book, *Why Am I Afraid to Tell You Who I Am?* says,

> . . . being a person necessarily implies becoming a person in process . . . my person is not a little hard core inside of me, a little fully-formed statue that is real and authentic, permanent and fixed: person rather implies a dynamic process. In other words, if you knew me yesterday, please do not think it is the same person you are meeting today.*

This good news reminds us that people can and do change. We are able to enhance our natural abilities and to acquire new ones.

Personal growth may be nurtured through the mind, by discovering insights about oneself or the behavior of others; through the body, by becoming aware of emotions and physical sensations (running, yoga, improving nutrition); and through the spirit by encountering God or God in one another. Learning to identify, acknowledge, and appropriately express one's feelings is a vital part of training. The more people understand and accept themselves, the more they will be able to care for others. The more fully they develop their potentials, the more they will be able to give to others.

Improving Caring Skills

Learning caregiving skills is a central focus of the training process. People can acquire information that will improve their ability to provide care. The more they learn about illness, the grief process, aging, divorce, crisis intervention, and referral, the more helpful they are likely to become. Improving caring skills may also require changing one's values, ways of thinking, belief systems, and assumptions about life and people.

Caregivers need a high degree of personal flexibility, especially when they are quite different from those they help. The ability to risk is essential for learners, who must be open to self-scrutiny and confrontation from others. Stereotypes must be discarded, assumptions challenged, and judgments abandoned. By learning when it is appropriate to share personal struggles, caregivers avoid burdening those in need with their own problems. For example, the woman who distrusts doctors because of a previous unfortunate experience needs to be aware of her feelings and biases if she is calling on a hospitalized person whose doctor has recommended surgery for the following day.

Learners have to forsake their need to be right and sometimes even their need to be helpful. Being close to another person often challenges our view of the world, people, and God. When we begin a relationship with someone, we risk being changed ourselves, sometimes in ways beyond our imagination. Caregivers must be able to flow with an unfamiliar situation, to live through the anxiety of not knowing what to do or how to respond to a hurting person. We need to learn when to plod on in faith, even if our work is unappreciated or possibly even resented, and when to stop offering help.

As a caregiver explores various options with someone in need, new personal possibilities may emerge. This can be both exciting and frightening. Personal defenses may be challenged. A strong, healthy woman who takes her health for granted may reconsider when she visits a twenty-year-old woman with cancer. The intellectual man who habitually hides his feelings may be shocked to discover his own tears as he holds the hand of a frightened child. Training should provide a loving, accepting environment for caregivers as they struggle with the changes occurring within themselves.

Integrating Theological Beliefs and Concepts into the Practice of Caregiving

"Theology forged on the anvil of personal experience is the best foundation for ministering to people."* The ministries of lay caregivers will be based on their theology and personal religious experience, even if these are born out of doubt and confusion. Learners often feel awkward or incompetent as they struggle with their "pastoral identity" and assume the responsibilities of pastoral care. Other important tasks of learning are to clarify and expand theological understandings and to integrate new religious insights, beliefs, and experiences into the practice of caregiving.

Five ways of assisting in this process may be mentioned.

Identifying the Theological Perspective

All events and relationships have implicit theological components. When a caregiver chooses to go to a weekly training session and misses a friend's birthday party, the elements of sacrifice and commitment are present. Being with people in pain is not easy; yet lay pastors do this week after week. As they learn to recognize and affirm the theological aspects of who they are and what they are doing, they may become more integrated themselves. The spiritual may not seem so distant and unknown.

Understanding the Nature of Human Beings

No single theory of personality has the power of the simple statement "We are all children of God." Recognizing this truth can change the way we relate to even the most difficult person. The learner's patience with a frustrating parishioner may affirm his or her recognition of that person as a Child of God.

Affirming Theological Motivation

Personal theological beliefs often sustain learners when they are in difficult situations in their ministries. Caregivers sometimes are not in touch with the religious part of their motivation when they ask themselves, "What am I doing visiting in this nursing home when I could be out on the golf course?" As they recognize the spiritual dimension of their motivation, they may feel better about their decision.

Enabling Recognition of a Power Beyond the Self

Sometimes lay pastors need to be strengthened and supported as they perform the difficult task of ministry. They often are nurtured by a power beyond themselves in ways that they do not recognize. These experiences can be affirmed, labeled, and celebrated. Some people find their strength through worship, by praying or reading the Bible; others, by sharing with loving friends or family. Some find time alone in quiet woods a source of strength. Still others re-create by running through the park. Whatever the means, caregivers may be encouraged to find ways to get in touch regularly with that source of power.

Proclaiming a Theology of Hope

Perhaps the most important endeavor is to help instill or nurture a sense of hope in the learners. As caregivers participate in human pain and alienation, they wrestle with themselves, their ministries, and their lives. A faith that provides a pervading and overriding sense of hope helps them continue their endeavors and adds richness and joy to their beings.

> The light shines in the darkness
> And the darkness has never put it out.
> —John 1:5 TEV

Learners' Responsibility for Their Own Education

We believe that a program for training lay caregivers should be designed around the principle that the learners are responsible for their own education. We have found this to be by far the most difficult concept for learners to understand and accept. It is also a most valuable one once they have grasped it.

The people who have been in training with us have included a wide span of educational backgrounds, interpersonal skills, and personal investment. Several people had doctoral degrees, but some had not completed high school; there were experienced social workers, and others who found a whole new world in the art of communicating; many people totally immersed themselves in the training, and a few gave a minimum of their time and interest. Their learning needs have been vastly different.

Caring is a highly personal endeavor. Learning to be a caregiver requires far more than becoming familiar with a few techniques or an established set of responses. What each caregiver needs to learn "evolves out of the problems workers encounter in the helping process,"* and these are different for each person. We believe that learners must decide what they want and need to learn, and assume major responsibility for making this learning happen.

This concept is easier to state than to put into practice. Learners sometimes become angry if we do not assume the role of an authoritative teacher or instructor who has definite answers. An attitude of "Why aren't you telling me the 'in secrets' of pastoral care?" seems to prevail. No matter how often we point out that we too struggle in difficult pastoral work and that there are no set scripts to follow, the attitude persists. The level of anger and frustration can become uncomfortable for all. We have had difficulty at times resisting a tendency to tell learners what to do and say, especially when they appear helpless.

Learner: The person I am calling on in the hospital has been moved to intensive care. What should I do?

Pastor: [Resisting the urge to give instructions] What do you think would be best?

Learner: [Becoming frustrated] How should I know? I'm not a minister! I don't know whether I'm allowed to go up there or even whether I should.

Pastor: Suppose you were not in a training program, and this person was a neighbor of yours. What would you do then?

Learner: I'd go see him.

Pastor: Why?

Learner: Because it's the thing to do. [Reconsidering] Because I would want him to know I care.

Pastor: And if you couldn't get into intensive care?

Learner: I'd write him a note, or send a card, or phone him. Maybe I'd talk to his family.

Pastor: How is this situation different?

Learner: Well, I guess it isn't. But I thought maybe there was a certain way we were supposed to do things.

Simply telling the learner to go would have been much easier. However, allowing learning caregivers to struggle even with the most obvious questions affirms their capacity and responsibility for their own learning. This is difficult for those who need to be "the teacher" or "the authority." You can help most by trusting the creative experience of each caregiver and his or her ability to grow and change. They will not disappoint you if you can be patient and supportive through the difficult times and find ways to handle your own frustration. As learners grow in confidence by actually making pastoral calls and discussing their experiences with one another, they begin to recognize their strengths and abilities and to trust their resources and skills.

Individual Goal Setting

Early in the training program the learners are asked to reflect upon their individual strengths, weaknesses, interests, and abilities and to formulate their individual goals for the training period. These are written down and then discussed in individual conferences. Learners are asked to be as specific as possible. Although this task may sound simple, it usually is difficult, especially if a person has had little experience in formal goal-setting.

Your task is to help the learner clarify goals and establish a realistic learning contract for the training program. This goal-setting is an evolving process. As a learner grows in self-understanding and experience, the goals may change or be expanded. Goals are individual and often differ considerably from one person to another. One beginning caregiver's goal might be to learn how to listen better. Others might see their goal as understanding their own feelings about death so that they can visit in nursing homes more comfortably.

Group Sharing of Individual Goals

After the learners' goals have been discussed in individual conferences, a group session in which goals are shared is helpful. This permits participants to copy from one another (a unique educational experience) and to offer suggestions to one another on specific ways to implement their goals. Books, workshops, or resource people may be recommended. Suggestions might be as simple as "My sister works with hyperactive children and can talk with you about how their problems affect a family" or "I have the book *Widow* by Lynn Caine,* which you may borrow." A powerful learning experience can happen when the group knows what a person wants to learn and is able to participate in the learning process.

Sylvia Houghton knew that sometimes she talked too much. She recognized that this usually happened when she was anxious or when she met new people. Sylvia set a goal for herself to learn to stop "over-talking." This goal was difficult because her hospital-calling assignment required that she meet new people. She was especially anxious because she wanted to do well in her ministry, and she knew that her tendency to fill silences with words could inhibit her effectiveness. Sylvia had a warm relationship with the people in her supervisory group. Although she felt vulnerable, she asked others in the group to help her. This gave them the invitation to confront her when she talked inappropriately.

Ongoing Process of Self-evaluation

Learners are not only responsible for setting goals but for periodically checking on their progress. This can be accomplished in several ways. Structured activities such as a midterm evaluation meeting can be provided. Learners may be asked to write their own progress reports, which will be shared with you and other group members. Learners are encouraged to state specifically the ways that they see each other growing and progressing.

Often learners will view you as "the teacher" and want to receive a grade. This is probably the least helpful way for them to evaluate their progress. The more a person can say, "I am learning," by remembering specific examples, the more meaningful the evaluation. "Ah ha!" experiences signal new awarenesses: "I didn't talk too much even though I felt uncomfortable when Arlene began to cry." "I helped Peter Jacobs express his feelings of loneliness yesterday." "Somehow I managed to answer with appropriate restraint when Susan English dumped on me her years of anger at the church." Such insightful recognitions are extremely important. As caregivers reflect on their learning experiences, they grow in confidence, begin to value their competence, and feel more autonomous in their ministries.

The Final Evaluation, which is written by the learner, helps to integrate the many learning experiences. Tracing the progress made and recognizing the growth that has occurred can be affirming. This evaluation examines the learner's relationship with the person or persons in need, the peer group, and the supervisor. The learner assesses personal strengths and areas in which more work or concentration is needed. Writing this final evaluation also helps learners express their feelings about ending this powerful learning commitment.

Learning Through Experience

Learning by Doing

Learning how to swim or ride a bicycle by exclusively reading a book or listening to a lecture is difficult to imagine. Some activities, including pastoral care, are learned best by doing.

Acquiring factual information, of course, is an important way to learn, but, because experience is such a vital way to learn, we have given it a primary place in our training model.

We have learners visit parishioners immediately after the weekend retreat. When this assignment is made, we are often barraged with questions: "Should I telephone first? What should I do if they can't come to the door? Can you give me more information about them? When is the best time to go? What do I do if they ask me to pray? Do they know I'm coming?" These questions reflect the anxiety of the learners, their feelings of inadequacy, and fear of the unknown. Making the pastoral visit answers most of these questions and helps learners overcome the unsettling feelings as well. Having gone, they feel more competent to visit again, and in the process they collect real-life data to reflect upon and share with other learners. An experience is worth ten thousand words.

Dialogue Between Theory and Practice

Training does not exclude examining the theory of pastoral care. Learning should be a dialogue between theory and practice: What is learned in theory should prove true to the learners' experience in caregiving, and caregivers should understand their experience better in light of the theoretical knowledge they acquire.

Learners are encouraged to try out the new caregiving skills they have learned in the training seminars. Help-giving relationships require that caregivers have more varied selections of responses than those needed for day-to-day living. Beginning caregivers tend to respond in a few favorite ways. Those caregivers who prefer to avoid anger or disruption probably will have difficulty in ministering to angry persons. Those who are inclined to be action-oriented and logical may become impatient with parishioners who avoid making decisions. Caregivers need to practice new ways of responding. As they begin to try different ways in their calling and in their relationships with others, they are encouraged to discuss these with one another. If the new responses were not successful, together they may explore why the situations were disappointing and try to create different, more effective approaches.

Caring about another sometimes involves listening and responding in a nurturing way even when we may disagree with or disapprove of what the person is saying or doing. Accepting a person without being judgmental is usually a challenge. Experiential learning can help caregivers understand that certain areas or subjects prompt judgmental attitudes on their part. We often judge others harshly when they remind us of parts of ourselves that we do not like. Caregivers can identify what they find offensive about another's behavior and apply that to themselves. This introspection, and the acceptance that caregivers experience within a caring group, can lead to personal growth and help them become more accepting of others and of themselves.

The unique personal histories of each of us can be an incredible source of learning, growing, and healing when shared appropriately with another. The widow who has survived and grown from grief, the parent who copes well with a handicapped child, the man who lost his job and changed careers in mid-life, the woman who begins a challenging educational pursuit in her later years—all have their stories to tell. Their personal "deaths and resurrections" can be inspirational and help instill hope in others. Sharing personal experiences in the training sessions can help caregivers learn when and how their unique gifts can be helpfully shared in caring situations.

Reflection and Evaluation

Learners also grow in their caregiving abilities by thinking about their experiences and making value judgments about what has occurred.

Role Playing

Role play or "reality practice" is a good way to help lay pastors practice caregiving skills with a minimum of risk. In a role play the beginning caregiver can make the most blatant errors and learn from them without worrying about disastrous effects on a person in need. In this way a group of learners can benefit from the helpful and "less than helpful" interventions that occur within a specific practice situation.

Beginners often feel threatened when they are asked to be in this kind of reality practice. This feeling is reduced when the activity is conducted in a warm accepting group of people who have had positive experiences together. When you first introduce a practice situation, you will need to provide more structure than will be required as participants become more familiar with this learning method. A role play should be stopped before the action becomes slow or boring. Participants are encouraged to get into their roles and not worry about how they are doing. Affirming the value of learning from errors and maintaining a "playful" attitude toward this method encourages participation.

Role playing is especially helpful before caregivers make their initial pastoral calls and experience high anxiety about actually knocking on the doors of other parishioners. As different "first call" roles are presented to the group, learners begin to realize that many different approaches and styles can be helpful and that one "right" way does not exist. As caregivers actively practice pastoral calls, this learning becomes part of their experience.

Observers can also learn from the discussions that follow a reality practice. Important questions to consider are:

1. How did the actors feel within their roles?
2. What events prompted emotional responses from them?
3. How would observers have done things differently? Why?
4. How realistic was the situation?
5. What did participants and observers learn?

Because role playing may elicit strong feelings in the participants, you must be sure that actors drop their roles after the discussion and reflection process has ended. One helpful way to accomplish this is to ask participants how they are different from the persons they were playing in the role. If they are similar, help them discover the subtle ways in which they are different or the ways in which they would like to be different. A strong focus on the "here and now" is helpful and can be accomplished by a simple statement like "Well, this is not a hospital room but our meeting room with its comfortable green chairs, and here we are together." After discussion has ended, a short break or a change-of-pace activity that requires movement is usually welcome.

Written Reports

Writing is another useful way to learn because it helps to clarify thoughts and serves as a recorded history of insights, questions, and feelings. For years people have recognized the value of keeping journals and diaries as a way of increasing their self-understanding and expressing their feelings.

Written reports are valuable in several ways. Learners grow in self-understanding as they describe the events and their feelings during particular pastoral calls. As they consider specific interactions that occurred with persons in need, they usually obtain a deeper understanding of those persons. Written reports also provide pictures of how the caregivers and the ones being helped relate with one another. These pictures add to your understanding of the learners and of the care being given, which in turn permits you to enhance the learning process. As caregivers share their written reports, they learn from a variety of real pastoral experiences and can offer suggestions and impressions to one another.

One of the simplest forms of clinical writing is a brief (or not so brief, depending on the learner) Weekly Report that describes a pastoral call, the feelings of the caller, and the interaction between the helper and the one receiving help. This report may contain a brief summary of verbal exchanges and general impressions formulated by the caregiver. It also aids in the learner's ongoing self-evaluation.

The Verbatim Report is, as nearly as possible, a word-for-word account of a pastoral care incident. A description of how the person looked or sounded may be included. A short history of the caregiver's ministry with that person introduces the actual verbatim account. The final section analyzes the verbal exchanges, evaluates what has happened, and poses questions for discussion. If group members have copies of the verbatim report a few days before it is presented, they are able to help the presenter by asking meaningful questions and offering observations and impressions.

Importance of Confidentiality

No discussion of clinical writing is complete without a statement about confidentiality. The real names of those receiving care are never used. Learners are encouraged to change nonessential identifying data in both written and oral reports. Even though names are not used, writers are asked to be extremely cautious with these reports and to be sure they are not read by anyone outside the training program. They are asked to treat the written reports like histories of their own most personal experiences.

Caring Community of Learners

The caring community that develops among learners is a crucial part of the learning experience. We have found the ideal group size to be four to seven people. Initiating the program with a weekend retreat provides a strong beginning to the important task of building relationships and establishing trust. During the course of weekly meetings the group gives much of the support, nurture, and encouragement necessary to sustain the learners in their caregiving and learning efforts. An atmosphere that is safe, trusting, and open enables learners to risk self-disclosure and to present their work for critical review. Within the group, members develop an ability to see and evaluate their strengths and weaknesses and to hear and accept the confrontations of the "truth in love" that facilitate growth and learning.

Within the context of the group, learners examine their ways of thinking, feeling, and behaving, all with the freedom to ask, "Is this the best way for me to do this? Is this really what I believe? Is this the way I want to be?" They gain a new perspective of themselves and their faith by seeing themselves through the eyes of others. Using the same evaluative eyes, they can view different attitudes, approaches, and belief systems that may challenge their own and that they may borrow or adopt if they wish. The group is a safe testing ground for trying new ways of behaving and being.

Learners find a "corrective" culture to heal old hurts and nurture growth that may have been stunted. For instance, some learners may have difficulty trusting others or recognizing and expressing feelings of anger or affection or connecting theological concepts such as grace, salvation, and forgiveness with real events in their lives. Because the group is a new community, its members are free to experience themselves and others in new ways and to form new patterns of being and caring for others. Caregivers learn how to minister effectively to those in need through their experiences of receiving care and support.

As friendships are formed, trusting relationships established, and intimacy generated, the group becomes a laboratory for learning, for loving, and for living. Bearing one another's burdens, they become a caring community for each other as they learn to provide pastoral care.

7. Supervising the Training

Quis custodes ipsos custodiet?
("Who takes care of those who take care?")*
—Ekstein and Wallerstein

Much of the pastor's work is done alone, especially in small churches. We suggest that from the very beginning you include others in training lay caregivers. When others design and plan a program for the church with you, the creativity of different people who have different perspectives is nourished and the base of congregational understanding and support is broadened.

We have found co-leadership to be extremely helpful, and we strongly encourage you to find someone to share this task. Each person has a unique way of relating with learners, and each can bring a variety of skills and resources to learning. Participants then can benefit from the professional and personal experiences of more than one person. Male and female co-leaders offer a well-rounded perspective and a leadership role model for both women and men.

Perhaps a community mental health worker, psychiatric nurse, physician, graduate student in a helping profession, pastor colleague, or other person skilled in human relationships can be recruited to share training responsibilities with you. If no such specially skilled or trained person is available, an interested friend, spouse, or another pastor should be enlisted to listen, encourage, support, and consult with you regularly.

The pastor's role in training lay caregivers can be summed up in the word "supervision." Supervision is a distinct form of ministry that draws upon your various skills as teacher, administrator, theologian, counselor, and caregiver. The shape of this distinctive ministry will vary according to the strengths and emphases of each pastor or co-supervisor. Supervision is a complex form of ministry involving a perspective, a task, a relationship, and a process.

The Perspective of Supervision

Supervision does not mean superiority but alludes to the pastor's perspective as one who has an "overseeing" vantage point. As a supervisor, the pastor is responsible for keeping an eye on the whole and for seeing separate events and interactions as a part of the ongoing learning process. By keeping track of individual threads, the supervisor may begin to see emerging patterns and offer learners a broader view. By maintaining an overall perspective (being "in the world but not of the world"), the pastor has an independent point of view. The supervisor is a participant in a helping process, but the primary focus of supervision is on the learning* that occurs, not on the pastoral care given to the caregiver or to the parishioner in need. As each issue arises, the pastor's first question from a supervisory perspective is "How does this relate to the caregiver's learning?"

Betty agonized with her supervisory group for nearly half an hour about the difficulty she was having finding child care for her son so that she could make her first assigned visit to the hospital. None of the many suggestions offered to her seemed to quell her uneasiness about leaving the child. Someone pointed out that Betty had not appeared upset when she left him to go to a movie a few weeks before. As she acknowledged this, the pastor wondered, "What does this have to do with Betty's learning to be a caregiver?" Betty soon revealed that she was feeling quite uneasy about going on her visits alone. Others in the group echoed her sentiments. Betty felt relieved and supported knowing that she was not the only one who felt anxious about the new ministry. This gave her confidence, and she remarked, "Oh, well, I can always leave the baby at my sister's."

By maintaining the supervisory perspective, you are free of the entanglement of the learners' personal problems and can be more helpful with the problems they face in learning to be caregivers. Without this perspective, a pastor might slip into a more familiar role of preacher, teacher, or counselor, to the neglect of some important learning issues.

The Task of Supervision

Providing Structure

The task of supervision is to provide the structure necessary for learning to take place. This includes designing the program, recruiting and screening participants, arranging for the retreat, setting times and places for weekly meetings, presenting seminars, and related duties. Although these may appear to be administrative, they are supervisory because the decisions made affect the caregivers' learning. Making assignments for visitation, for instance, is not simply a matching of people by age, interest, or geographic proximity. A supervisor decides whom each caregiver will visit by evaluating the several learners' abilities and reflecting on what they want and need to learn.

Creating an Atmosphere for Learning

Part of the structure necessary for learning is an atmosphere that is open, trusting, and safe. Supervisors can help to create a positive group experience by encouraging risk-taking and appropriate self-disclosure, by promoting acceptance of mistakes as a valuable resource for learning, and by celebrating growth and learning as they occur. You can contribute much toward this by being warm, accepting, and caring, and by sharing your humanness. Supervisors greatly influence the perimeters of what is acceptable, for instance, by how they respond to tardiness and absenteeism and by how they stress the importance of trust and confidentiality.

Dealing with Feelings

A primary task of supervision is to help learners recognize

and talk about their feelings. Understanding how other persons feel is one major part of caring for them. The first step in learning to understand someone else's feelings is to be in touch with your own.

A helpful suggestion for beginning supervisors is to "look, listen, and feel." More specifically, watch the learners, observe what they do, listen to what they say, and know what you are feeling. When you feel anxious, chances are good that many of the learners share that feeling. If you feel that something important is happening, you're probably right. If you feel bored, something important probably is being avoided. You as a person, your senses, feelings, perceptions, and hunches, are your greatest asset. Being aware of these aspects of your self can help you use the knowledge you have and also help you to acquire more through your experiences. Most people ordinarily are not pushed to look at their feelings, at least not to the same extent that they are in a training program, so some resistance is to be expected. You can be helpful to caregivers by sharing your feelings (which may not be much different from theirs) and by assuring them that their discomfort is natural and to be expected.

You may increase your awareness of what learners are feeling by using the "here and now" approach. This means that you listen to all discussions and incidents described to you as supervisor as if they have some relation to what people are feeling at the present moment. What people talk about, even if it is an event of the past, may provide some clue about how they are currently feeling.

Lynn Kristy visited Debbie Bitner, who was in the midst of a divorce and had recently begun a new job. Debbie was polite but formal with Lynn and shared very little of herself and her feelings. Lynn was unusually quiet in her supervisory group but, after a bit of coaxing, shared her visit.

Lynn: I know Debbie must be almost bursting with all that's going on in her life, but she's keeping it locked up inside. That's not like her at all.

Supervisor: What do you suppose Debbie is feeling?

Lynn: Nervous, overwhelmed. Probably guilty and frustrated that she can't handle all that she has to do. Debbie is a person who likes to do things well.

Supervisor: Do you recall ever feeling that way yourself?

Lynn: [Thinks for a moment, then laughs uncomfortably] Sometimes I feel like that in here. This is all so new to me, and there's so much to learn. I want to do well, and I'm afraid if I tell you about it you'll see everything I did wrong. Sometimes I'd rather not say anything!

Several others in the group said they were feeling the same way. A lively discussion about trust and acceptance followed, and Lynn gained new insight about herself and her pastoral situation.

Lynn: I'll bet Debbie might be reluctant to talk about those feelings too, especially on the first visit. Maybe if I didn't try so hard, we'd both do better.

Listening for parallels between what is being said about the person visited and what is being felt by the caregiver often helps the supervisor understand what learners are experiencing. Frequently a particular feeling of one group member is shared by other learners. One question to ask yourself again and again is "Why is this person making this statement at this time to this person in this manner?"*

Keeping Learners on the Track

Learning pastoral care requires that caregivers look at their mistakes, involve themselves in others' pain, wrestle with their feelings, and struggle with theological issues. This is a difficult and sometimes agonizing effort. Understandably (and often unconsciously), learners may try to avoid this task.

Caregivers have some favorite ways to keep from learning:

1. Wandering off the subject. (They are usually most successful in this when they choose a topic that interests the supervisors.)
2. Dealing with learning material "in theory" only.

("What would happen if I were to visit twice in one week?" "How do we really know that a man who lost his job is anxious or depressed?")

3. Getting stuck on details or procedure. (Learners may avoid their feelings about writing verbatims by arguing about whether these reports should be typed, by discussing how long they should be, or by debating when they should be handed in.)
4. Bringing up real problems that have no relations to the learning issue except to distract from it. ("My brother in St. Louis called me the other night, and he has some serious personal problems I'd like to discuss.")

Learners are quite creative in their ability to divert supervisors from the learning task. We have often found ourselves feeling as if we were following a killdeer attempting to distract us by a feigned injury when the real nest egg lay near by. When you are feeling restless, impatient, or bored or when you are very much interested but find yourself asking, "What does all this have to do with learning pastoral care?" you probably are being led off the track.

One of the encouraging and reassuring parts of being a supervisor is that you have more than one chance to identify the learning issues of a group. If something important happens and you miss it, you will have another opportunity to be helpful, because the important issues keep appearing over and over.

The Supervisory Relationship

Supervising the learning of lay caregivers requires a definite change in the relationship between pastor and parishioner. As a supervisor, you will relate differently to your church members as learners because your role in relation to them has changed.

If Jill says to a friend, "I really feel rotten today," she may expect some sympathy and comfort. If she happens to be in an examining room and the friend is her physician, she will expect something more than "Aw, that's too bad. I hope you feel better tomorrow." When they encounter you as a supervisor, your parishioners may not expect "something different" from you. They may be confused or upset by your new role. We always discuss this change directly with our learners, especially if we have close friends among them. Pastors in smaller churches may struggle more with this change of role because they are more likely to have well-established relationships with all the caregivers.

The differences between pastor and supervisor are usually less subtle than at first imagined. These differences may be seen most clearly by contrasting supervisory and pastoral responses.

Parishioner: I spoke with Carolyn in the hospital this morning. She just can't understand why God did this to her. I didn't know what to say.

As a Pastor: That is a tough question. I'm sorry she's having such a bad time. I appreciate your letting me know. I'll stop by to see her this afternoon.

As a Supervisor: That sounds like good pastoral care. Carolyn is trusting you with some important theological issues. How did you handle that? How might you have done it differently?

Parishioner: When we signed up for this course, we expected you to show us what to do and how to do it. We want some answers!

As a Pastor: I'm very sorry, there seems to be some misunderstanding. The Christian Education Committee outlined the course very clearly in the brochure. Is there anyone else who feels the way Mike does? Perhaps we can make some adjustments so that this course can be more satisfying for everyone.

As a Supervisor: Yes, Mike. Not having specific answers and procedures is frustrating for me too sometimes. How does this method affect your learning?

Parishioner: How many people would like to change the meeting time to 7:30? Good. How's that for you, pastor?

As a Pastor: My calendar is open. If it's more convenient

for everyone else, I don't see why we shouldn't change.

As a Supervisor: Sure, I can change, but I wonder if the time is really the issue here. What do you think?

You can participate most fully and productively in the caregivers' learning if they see you as a helper, supporter, and co-learner. The more the learners can trust that you are on their side, the more they can invite you to look with them at their mistakes and bring to you their "unacceptable" feelings. If they see you as a partner in their learning, they can hear your confrontations and accept your challenges. As we looked back on our training experiences, we decided, in the beginning stages, to schedule more individual conferences in order to build a strong alliance with each learner. Opening one's self and one's work to scrutiny is a threatening experience. When we are vulnerable and open about our humanness, learners experience us as supportive partners with them in their journey to become competent, compassionate caregivers.

As supervisors we need to examine our part of the relationship with our learners and then work on ourselves in order to enhance the learning. One of the advantages of working as a team is that we can ask one another, "Am I causing problems in the learning?" Sometimes the answer is yes. We then try to figure out what is happening with us. If you find yourself having difficulty with a particular learner, you may ask yourself, "Does she remind me of someone else?" or "Do I ever act like her?" Perhaps that person reminds you of someone you do not like or are angry with, or of a part of yourself that you are displeased with. Once you recognize what your part of the problem is, it is easier to change. Anyone who decides to be a participant in another's growth and learning needs to be prepared to grow and learn.

To declare that learners are responsible for their own education does not relieve supervisors of all responsibility in the learning process. Supervision is neither dictatorial control nor detached observation but the investment of one's self in a relationship. Supervisors "can evoke the initiative and responsibility of others only by risking and involving" their own.* As a supervisor, your authority comes not from how much you know or see or understand or believe but from how well you can help the caregivers learn what they need to know. This involves "the transcending of rules and games" and the sharing of self "without a need for there to be a winner or a master player."* As the relationship evolves, supervision becomes less what you *do*, and more who you *are* for the caregiver. For many, you will become a cherished partner in a rare journey of becoming.

The Process of Supervision

Supervision also may be seen as a process that has, to some degree, a predictable history. Aspects of the process deserve to be highlighted.

Clarifying and Establishing a Contract

Learners and supervisors bring to the training program expectations that are often quite different. From the moment they first hear of its existence learners may begin to imagine what a training program might be like for them. If they decide to apply and participate, their initial expectations and fantasies often become part of an unstated contract that they hope will be fulfilled. Likewise you as supervisor have a certain preunderstanding about how learning will occur. Your expectations should be stated directly as you design and promote a training program. No matter how clear you attempt to be, however, you, too, will have implied contracts that need to be clarified. The more the implied contracts of both learners and supervisors can be recognized and stated, mutually negotiated and agreed upon, the more smoothly the learning will progress. Although the collaborative process is an ongoing one and complete clarification is impossible, we encourage you to be as clear and open as you can about what you hope and expect, especially in the beginning stages of training.

The application and screening procedures that we use are designed to help in the process. For example, when we ask interested persons to apply and complete written applications, we are demonstrating that we value the personal learning experience and that we expect learners to look at themselves and be willing to share their insights in writing. We ask them to be self-revealing and to trust us to be helpful to them in their learning, and we also are willing to be self-revealing.

The screening interview is a further way of showing that we expect the learners to be responsible for their own learning. It raises these kinds of questions:

1. What do *you* want to know about this training program?
2. What do *you* think *you* need to learn to become a more effective caregiver?
3. How might we be helpful to *you* in *your* learning?

If an applicant says, "I thought you would tell me all about the program," we have a chance to explain our part of the contract. The person who is extremely uncomfortable with this approach will probably decide not to continue or may express doubts, which can then be discussed. In either case the contract has been clarified.

When caregivers decide to commit themselves to a training program, they agree to certain expectations that are part of that commitment or contract. For instance, they must be willing to attend a weekend retreat and the twelve training sessions and to make at least one pastoral call a week during the training period. We commit ourselves to provide learning experiences for them, to participate in their learning by sharing ourselves and our skills, and to provide the structure in which the learning can take place.

Encouraging Beginners

Many people have a difficult time assuming the role of learners because they are used to being "knowledgeable" in their work as teachers, managers, homemakers, physicians, or shop stewards. Some may feel especially helpless because they expect themselves to remain "the expert" but realize that pastoral care is unfamiliar territory. Others may feel inadequate because they have been away from organized learning programs or vocational experiences for several years. Beginning caregivers often lack confidence in their ability and behave as if they have no resources of their own. Although they are competent adults with many skills, they may feel helpless because of their anxiety about the unknown.

You can help learners affirm their abilities as individuals and as a group by asking them to recall times when they were able to cope effectively with similar situations. Sharing your past feelings of anxiety about a particular pastoral call or your present anxiety about beginning a training program can assure them that someone else has felt the way they do and still was able to be helpful to others. You might also demonstrate your confidence in them by reminding them that they were chosen to be in this program because they had shown that they could be helpful and that they were willing to learn new ways to be even more effective. All of these methods help caregivers realize that their anxiety is natural and temporary and will not interfere with their ministry in any lasting way.

Identifying Learning Issues

One of the primary purposes of a training program is to help caregivers discover what they want and need to learn in order to become more effective in their pastoral work. Learners tend to approach new learning situations in the same way that they have approached learning in the past. This is true whether the new situation is a group training session, an individual conference, or a pastoral call. As you discover learners' usual approaches, you can help them use these effectively in their calling or perhaps encourage them to try some different ways of learning.

Ekstein and Wallerstein* have described several common learning styles in a way that has been helpful to us in identifying learning issues for particular caregivers.

The Passive Learner

The passive learner ("Tell me what to do") is most easily recognized by her or his silence or lack of action. This person may wait for someone else to arrange transportation to a retreat, sit back while others volunteer for role plays, and expect the supervisor to set the agenda for an individual conference. Passive learners are usually pleasant and supportive. Although they do learn while they are being passive, they could learn much more if they would become more active in their learning. Passive learners are more likely to copy a supervisor's style rather than form one of their own. People can learn much by imitating, but the imitation limits the ways in which their unique gifts and rich life experiences could be used in their ministries. Passive learners are probably open to more active involvement. If they had wanted to stay passive they probably would not have entered a training program. After all, both learning and pastoral caring are active endeavors. Supervisors, then, can look for ways to encourage their assertiveness.

Gwen Gillam had been an excellent student in school and was looking forward to the training program for lay caregivers in her church. After her first meeting with her supervisor, Ed Ford, she felt confused, disappointed, and frustrated. She had asked Ed what books she should read and he, in turn, asked her what specific skills or knowledge she thought she needed to learn. She asked if she should telephone a parishioner before she visited, and he responded with a vague reply: "That's one way to begin." Much to Gwen's frustration he then added, "Have you thought of any others?" Throughout the interview Gwen persisted in her attempts to have Ed fit into her model of a good teacher. Ed wisely resisted and was understanding of Gwen's frustration. He knew that Gwen was a bright, creative woman, and he wanted to help her rely more on her own resources.

Several weeks later, Gwen realized that her former approach to learning was not getting her what she wanted, and she began to try out some of her own ideas instead of pirating Ed's. As she came to realize that many of these were indeed helpful, she was able to validate her own work. She had expanded her former learning style into one that was more autonomous and challenging.

The Great Debater

The great debater ("I disagree!") tends to challenge any new idea. If you suggest that no single procedure exists for an initial pastoral call, some learners may insist that there should be one.

If you suggest that caregivers should share feelings with parishioners, some learners will talk about the importance of focusing on problem-solving. All the while they are disagreeing, they may actually be considering the new idea—and arguing only in order to test its validity and assess its potential value. About the time you give up on them, they agree with you. Great debaters often learn a great deal without your knowing that they are learning at all. They are simply using a familiar pattern of challenging and questioning.

If you value this style, however impatient you may become with it at times, you will be surprised to discover that the learners may indeed have incorporated some new ideas into their ministry. Ask them to risk expanding their usual way of learning and try something new before they condemn it.

The Apologetic Learner

The apologetic learner ("I blew it again") will quickly agree with any challenge or confrontation. If you ask why such a person said something, the reply may be "I knew I shouldn't have said that." If you ask for a description of a pastoral visit, you may receive a response like "I was probably too pushy; that's one of my faults." Apologetic learners see the supervision as an attack and may defend themselves by finding fault before you can. You can be helpful to such persons by being especially supportive in the beginning and "joining" with them in their learning. Supporting their strengths and creativity is helpful. A sense of humor can also assist the learning. In a friendly, joking manner you might say something like "Now, Jack, before you tell me what you did wrong, tell me something you feel good about." Or "You have an excellent critical ability; that is a strength of yours. How about trying to develop the capacity to see what you did *right* too?" You might ask group members to respond to the self-criticism of the apologetic learners in order that they can hear what their approaches sound like to others.

The Denying Learner

The denying learner ("That's not important anyway") likes

to discount or devalue something he or she would prefer to avoid. Such persons may suggest, "I don't think we should visit the Wilsons; they have enough sorrow without us reminding them of it." Or they may stress the importance of "being objective" in order to avoid the frightening possibility of sharing intimately with another. Such people can be asked to imagine what might happen in a visit if they used a different approach; that sometimes helps them become aware of what is frightening them.

Supervisor: What would happen if you were not so objective?
Learner: They might get emotional and start to cry.
Supervisor: So?
Learner: What would happen if I cried too?
Supervisor: What would happen?
Learner: I'd feel embarrassed. After all, I am supposed to be the helper.
Supervisor: What might the parishioners think?
Learner: They'd probably think I really cared.
Supervisor: Would that be bad?
Learner: I guess not, but I sure get frightened when I think about it.

Working Yourself Out of a Job

The end of a training program is a time of loss. The greater the investment of the caregivers, the greater the loss. Yalom sees the end of a group as being "entirely analogous to the death of a loved one. . . . [It] may evoke memories of past losses."* Caregivers may try to deny the reality of ending in order to avoid the feelings of loss, sadness, and pain. They often say things like "This really isn't over, because we all can get together in a month or so." They may ask if you could continue weekly meetings, or if they could meet every other week without you. If you get caught up in extending a training program, you lose the opportunity to help caregivers learn from their grief and sense of loss.

A primary task of supervision at this time is to help caregivers deal with their feelings about the ending of the program. As they learn about endings they will become more helpful to parishioners who have experienced loss and will be better prepared to enable a good termination with their parishioners when that relationship ends. Learning about endings is important because "termination is, after all, a part of almost every relationship, and throughout one's life one must, on many occasions, say goodbye to important people."†

We use the topics of our weekly seminars to help in the process of ending. In the ninth of the twelve-seminar series we discuss aging and the losses that are often a part of that process. We also affirm the potential for new beginnings in the latter stages of life and speak of some of the advantages of having fewer responsibilities. In the tenth seminar we discuss loss and grief and how to minister to the grieving person. We present grief as a healthy process that has a beginning and an end. The eleventh seminar considers death and dying and focuses on the stages of death and on the needs of the dying person and his or her family. Personal experiences and beliefs about death are often shared. The twelfth seminar is on termination and is an experiential study of endings.

We believe that to enable a good termination of a training program a supervisor should provide the structure wherein the following tasks can be completed:

1. Review the group's history, with special emphasis on the learning and growth of individuals and of the group.
2. Express feelings of loss, regret, and appreciation.
3. Redefine the relationship between the learners and the supervisors.
4. Discover the gains in the loss—the resurrection in the death.
5. Celebrate the experience.

The structure that we use consists of a separate fina
view with each caregiver, a concluding group trair
sion designed to facilitate the completion of the tas
banquet to celebrate the sharing of a powerful anc
experience.

Review

The review of an individual caregiver's learning is done most extensively in the interview. Another way to facilitate this review is to ask group members to write brief evaluations of one another and share these in their last group meeting. A simple way to help members of a group review their history is to ask them to recall their experiences together and share significant events with one another.

Express Feelings

Both learners and supervisors need to express their feelings. Questions like "What will you miss?" "What do you wish you had done differently?" or "What was meaningful to you?" can be helpful. If you share your feelings of loss, regret, and appreciation, others usually begin to share theirs.

Redefine the Relationship

To begin redefinition of the relationship between learners and supervisor, the supervisor can make a direct statement like "Well, things will be different for us now that you won't be turning in weekly reports and I won't be commenting on them." An even more effective way for you to help this redefinition of roles is for you to drop your role as supervisor. You may assure them of your availability for consultation, but you are no longer responsible for identifying learning issues or for taking a different perspective. Once again you can simply be a pastor or friend. As you let go of your supervisory responsibilities, caregivers will recognize this and realize that the relationship has changed.

iscover the Gains

ne of the most important parts of termination is that of overing the gains in the loss. Caregivers have risked, , and learned and have been the caring community for hurch members and for one another. They gain a sense plishment, some relief, new skills, and often a new ng. You too will have learned and grown, and you will have gained several competent, compassionate caregivers to share with you the joys and challenges of pastoral care.

Celebrate

Celebration is a vital part of ending a training program. Caregivers have committed their time and energy to a challenging and demanding endeavor. The existence of this commitment and the accomplishments that have been achieved should be validated, appreciated, savored, and celebrated. You also will have reason to celebrate your commitment and your achievements.

The form or structure that you choose is not important. We usually have a dinner at the church. A concluding Communion service can be a meaningful and most appropriate way to end.

8. Summary

> The journey of a thousand miles
> begins with a single step.
> —Chinese Proverb

The same principles that help lay caregivers to learn can assist you as you create a training program. Begin with yourself—your personal growth, caring skills, and theology. Become a learner. Affirm your unique gifts and life experiences and be open to new ones. Learn to recognize the value of being vulnerable instead of being perfect. Realize that you will make mistakes and learn from them; you will survive them, and so will the lay caregivers.

Enlist others as co-workers to struggle, work, and learn with you. Together, examine the needs of the congregation, set goals, and explore how these might be implemented. Be responsible for your own learning; use our ideas and experiences to spark your own creativity. Your dreams of an active, caring community can become a reality.

One of the most caring things you can do for a church and for yourself is to enable others in caregiving. Putting theology into practice in this way can visibly change the whole life of a congregation. We believe that you will be awed and inspired by the gifts, talents, and commitment that lay people will bring to is mutual ministry.